"At a time when leadership i
insights for all on what it ta
acquired skill."
Paul Polman, CEO, Unilever

"Leaders should be readers and Eve Poole's Leadersmithing is a
must-read for anyone that wants to improve their ability to lead.
Whether you run a business, a small team, or aspire to lead in the
future, Leadersmithing will help you become the leader you want to be,
with strong practical insight, humour and honesty."
Jayne-Anne Gadhia, Chief Executive, Virgin Money

"I stumbled into leadership by accident rather than design. My learning
was all 'on the job' with many mistakes and a few successes. How much
easier my job would have been if there had been books like this around
to help me navigate my journey."
John Barton, Chairman, Easyjet and Next

"I found the book fascinating. Whether you are looking for leadership
advice when tackling a new challenge, or merely developing your
personal leadership skills, Eve's deck of cards will provide the
inspiration."
Major General Paul Nanson, Commandant, The Royal Military
Academy Sandhurst and Director Leadership for the British Army

"This is a leadership book from the frontline, written from a deep base
of academic understanding but grounded in the daily practice of the
leadership art. I will be buying it for all my Board and recommending
it very often"
Stephen Bampfylde, Chairman, Saxton Bampfylde

"This is a different kind of leadership book. It encourages and inspires.
It shows us that we all need to continue to learn and develop our
leadership skills, however high or low we may be. And it reminds us
that it's a journey of one step at a time, with a lot of work on the way.
It's a must-read."
Chris Smith, Baron Smith of Finsbury, Master of Pembroke College
Cambridge

"Inspirational, practical and fascinating, this book will help you no
matter what your age or achievements. I couldn't put it down."
Joanna Lumley

Leadersmithing

Leadersmithing

Revealing the Trade Secrets of Leadership

Eve Poole

Bloomsbury Business
An imprint of Bloomsbury Publishing Plc

B L O O M S B U R Y
LONDON · OXFORD · NEW YORK · NEW DELHI · SYDNEY

Bloomsbury Business

An imprint of Bloomsbury Publishing Plc

50 Bedford Square	1385 Broadway
London	New York
WC1B 3DP	NY 10018
UK	USA

www.bloomsbury.com

First published 2017

Reprinted 2018, 2019

British Library Cataloguing-in-Publication Data

A catalogue record for this book is available from the British Library.

ISBN: PB: 978-1-4729-4123-7
      ePDF: 978-1-4729-4124-4
      ePub: 978-1-4729-4121-3

Library of Congress Cataloging-in-Publication Data

A catalog record for this book is available from the Library of Congress.

Cover design by Dani Leigh
Cover image © iStock Images

Typeset by Fakenham Prepress Solutions, Fakenham, Norfolk NR21 8NN
Printed and bound CPI Group (UK) Ltd, Croydon, CR0 4YY

For all the leaders I have taught and coached, with thanks for sharing with me your confidences and your lack of confidence. I hope this book helps.

And for my godchildren, Daisy, Monty and Lulu.

Contents

How To Read This Book

Figure 1 How to read this book

This book is for anyone who wants to improve their own ability to lead or to help others to do so.

Perhaps you are a **leader in training**. Try scheduling all seventeen of the Critical Incidents or curating your own learning journey, using the self-assessment found in Appendix 3.

Are you a **leader transitioning** into a more senior role or changing career? Use Appendix 1 to work out what most scares you about your next step and to diary in some practice.

If you consider yourself to be an **emerging leader**, you might like to work your way through the exercises found in Part 2 of this book. How many Critical Incidents can you diary into your day job?

If you are **talent**, use Appendix 3 to nurture your strengths and overcome potential career blockers.

Are you a **weary leader**? Use the book to boost your energy, by focusing on where you feel least well resourced.

Perhaps you are already a **senior leader**. You might use the book to coach and mentor colleagues and to refresh your own practices.

If you are reading this as an **executive coach**, you might want to use the book with your clients to focus their development on where they most need resourcing.

If you work in **Learning and Development**, you may have a particular responsibility for nurturing leaders in your organization. This book will help you by providing a framework for you to audit your offer or to curate a fresh leadership curriculum.

Foreword

Over the years, I have been close to many leaders and watched them make that most difficult of transitions, to the C-suite. Whether CEO, CFO or any other C-level job, I have observed at close quarters how they managed, or failed, to grow into the position, for they surely weren't job-ready when they arrived. And that is exactly the purpose of this book. It aims to help executives to prepare in advance for the top job, to minimize the personal pain of transition and to maximize organizational effectiveness.

Eve Poole is correct in her assertion that there is very little written about what the C-level job actually entails. She starts by demystifying leadership and turning the position into a pragmatic job description. Once that is done, she offers advice on how to develop effective strategies for each of the seventeen job requirements. She brings alive the old adage, 'manage yourself, lead others' with down-to-earth exercises designed to help you to complete the apprenticeship before you take on the job.

Because the book is designed to be read in different ways, it is a helpful guide –whether you are a young leader just setting out on your career or already only a breath away from being the most senior leader. And, because it is based on a mixture of research and experience, it is a trustworthy guide.

Don't be fooled. Just because the advice is grounded and pragmatic that doesn't mean that this will be an easy apprenticeship. You still have to ask for feedback that you won't want to hear. You still have to deal with poor performers. You still have to motivate and inspire others. The buck will stop with you as the figurehead and you will have to have the courage to step out into the unknown and to take risks. None of this is simple or straightforward – among other things, it requires brutal self-honesty and lots of practice. You will have to take yourself less seriously and pay a lot more attention to others. But then, if you want to be a leader, you already know that you have to invest in the hard work of preparation. This book provides you with a clearer road map.

The bottom line is that it's all about learning. Not sticking with the same old bag of tricks, but discarding stuff that no longer works and adding new practices that do.

While learning to be an effective leader may be hard work, reading this book isn't. Eve bounces you along the storyline, with erudite references alongside amusing and practical anecdotes – Machiavelli's *The Prince* alongside *The Wizard of Oz*.

Leaders bear great responsibility. They are responsible for creating wealth that sustains prosperity and thus life. They wield huge power and can make the lives of their followers a joy or a misery. We always need more and better leaders. This book will help anyone who is serious about being a good leader to achieve that goal.

Dr Liz Mellon
Chair, editorial board of Duke CE journal,
Dialogue, and author of *Inside the Leader's Mind* (2011)

Introduction

Did you know that leadership books have been around for centuries? Julius Caesar, Genghis Khan and Elizabeth I would have read them – any leader of yore. They used to be written largely for kings and there were so many of them that the genre had a name: *principum specula*, or 'mirrors for princes'. All kinds of people wrote them, often to curry favour or to make a political point. One of them famously bombed: in 1513, Niccolò Machiavelli wrote *The Prince*, the book for which he is most known today, and it went down like a lead balloon. This was because it did not fit in with the genre at the time. Everyone else was writing moralistic leadership books that were heavy on theory and were generally about being heroic. Machiavelli, however, wrote his book about the harsh realities of rule, saying: 'since my intention is to say something that will prove of practical use to the inquirer, I have thought it proper to represent things as they are in a real truth, rather than as they are imagined' (Ch. XV). To his audience, it must have felt like a self-help book entitled *Pull Your Finger Out*. They were very cross and persuaded the Pope to ban the book, which, of course, made it an extremely hot ticket.

Not so many years later, a similar but more junior genre emerged, aimed at apprentices. Daniel Defoe's *The Complete English Tradesman* (1726) was one such book. Like those addressed to kings, these were usually moral tomes that exhorted good behaviour and obedience to the master. They were not detailed instruction manuals for individual trades: if authors had the temerity to write down anything practical, it looked suspiciously like the sharing of trade secrets and, as such, they were publicly condemned by their Guild.

Many modern leadership books follow these traditions. Often they assume their audience is chief executives and so are full of rousing stories about heroic leaders. They still do not really tell us what leaders need to do on a day-to-day basis. We remain transfixed by leaders who look the part, and become easily distracted by cerebral argument about what the word 'leadership' really means, rather than focusing on the detailed daily application of leader-craft.

I have spent over a decade teaching at Ashridge Business School, during which time I have taught and coached thousands of leaders. I have also conducted empirical research about what makes them tick and I want to demystify leadership to make it accessible to everyone. We need more and better leaders badly, at every level in organizations, and also in all walks of life.

Have you ever been on a leadership training course? I bet it started with a terribly serious conversation about whether leaders are born or made. Probably the conclusion was that it is a bit of both. Given the context, you were probably encouraged to believe that even if you were not precisely to the manner born, you might at least be able to make the most of whatever leadership skills you might possess, through the good offices of the person teaching you.

Might I guess at the next bit? I bet in the next exercise you were asked to name some famous leaders. Probably this included Winston Churchill, Nelson Mandela, Mother Teresa and Mahatma Gandhi. Possibly you included Richard Branson or another popular entrepreneur, as well. This was closely followed by a flip chart exercise about 'management' versus 'leadership', with all the old favourites about rule taking and rule making and so on.

If I were to give you a leadership exam, I bet you would all pass it. 100 per cent. Congratulations! Because the cognitive psychologists and moral philosophers think that right thought leads to right action, you should be sorted. In reality, though, leadership is simply not this theoretical. On-paper answers are not enough, particularly when you are in a panic. Leading is a very messy business and the trial and error of hard experience is a far better teacher than any guru in a classroom.

Remember, leaders are made, *not* born. Even those who seem to have been born into leadership cannot avoid having to show up and get through the various trials of office. Perhaps the traditional schooling of some key families had this baked in to their syllabus and lifestyle, which is why we thought leading was a birthright. But there is no mystery; it is no longer a closed shop. We know what leading involves and leadership is not the preserve of an elite. We need too much of it, too urgently, for it not to be fundamentally and radically democratized.

To me, the word 'leadership' itself is problematic. It feels more like title or status than an on-going activity. So I am going to call it 'leadersmithing', because it is about apprenticeship, craft and hours of practice.

What associations do you have with the word 'practice'? My guess is either panic about spelling or the ghost of childhood music lessons. Either way, Malcolm Gladwell's view that it takes 10,000 hours of practice to create mastery is very sobering. Luckily, when it comes to leadersmithing, I do not agree with him.

I was once given a very beautiful miniature marble font. It is an antique apprentice piece produced by a trainee stonemason to show that he was ready to graduate. By making something perfectly in miniature, he demonstrated that he was ready to be trusted with the big stuff. The selection of the right materials, the careful use of tools, the painstaking attention to detail, allowed him to create a tiny thing of beauty and usefulness. Because of my research into leaders and how they learn, I think that developing leaders is all about this kind of activity: the accelerated acquisition of skill in the foundational practices of leading.

What is the leadership equivalent of an apprentice piece? Ashridge produced a list of must-haves by asking senior leaders what they wish they had known earlier on in their careers. From what we know about neurobiology, the more emotionally charged the situation is in which these skills are acquired, the deeper the resulting memory and its retrievability under pressure in the future.

What we developed at Ashridge on the back of this research is a bit like a vaccine – the right kind of experience in the right dose to equip you to prevail when 'experience' comes knocking. You can curate this kind of learning for yourself. You just need to ask your own leaders or role models what they consider to be the best 'apprentice pieces' for leading, then schedule them into your day job, ideally under pressure. Or just write down everything that scares you about top leadership, line them in your sights and pick them off one-by-one until you know you are job-ready.

This book shows you how. Part 1 is all about theory. First, we will look at the cheat-sheet for what leaders need to be able to do. I will tell you about our recipe research, where we answered this question retrospectively by asking board-level leaders 'what do you know now as a leader that you wish you had known ten years ago?' Next, I will tell you what we can learn from this and from subsequent neurobiological research, about how leaders actually learn. Do we really need to practise it for 10,000 hours, or are there any short-cuts? Then, before I explain what I mean by 'leadersmithing', I will summarize my findings by discussing the importance of character. And leadersmithing itself? It is all about craft and mastery, and the importance of apprentice-pieces.

Part 2 is about practice and I will spend the rest of the book offering you a whole year's worth of crafty essentials, to help you design your own development as a leader, week by week, until you are templated to cope with everything we know leaders need to be able to do. And the great thing about this book is that you do not need to read it all. Figure 1 (see page x) offers you a menu for how to read the book. Generally, you may prefer theory; in which case, read the first half. Or you may prefer practice; so, read the second. Or start with the winning hands in Appendix 1 and the self-assessment in Appendix 3. Or just pick your favourite word from the index and go from there.

Part one

Theory

Chapter 1

What Do Leaders Need to be Able to Do?

Leadership 101

You have probably sat through more than your fair share of talks about leadership. But in case it helps as a reminder up front, here is a refresher on the history of thinking about leadership. In 2015, the National Gallery in London, hosted a series of events called *Life Lessons from the Old Masters*. I teamed up with their Head of Education, Gill Hart, to deliver the session on 'Leadership'. I kicked it off by using three of the gallery's famous paintings to tell the story.

First, I spoke about Goya's portrait of the Duke of Wellington. Have you ever thought about where 'leadership' really came from, as a topic? Research into the subject became urgent as Europe ran out of leaders after the First World War. Much of it was funded by the military, so it is unsurprising that this first wave of thought-ware was all about the leader as hero, triumphant in battle and a fine figure of a man. Wellington was so heroic that he kept winning medals and Goya subsequently had to add them into his portrait. Wellington epitomizes the heroic leader and appeals to organizations which prize competition and market share, because this narrative is all about beating the opposition. We still have not lost this model, which is why taller men – and men in general – are paid more, and why dynasties remain important in many walks of life, because of notions about the officer class.

Next, Holbein the Younger's *The Ambassadors*, which shows two fabulously dressed pillars of the community, surrounded by artefacts and symbols of their education and power. As technology made warfare less about cannon fodder and more about strategy, we began to look for leaders with brains, as well as brawn. *The Ambassadors* 'jaw-jaw, not war-war' represents this phase, which is epitomized today by the MBA culture and the lingering importance of the 'old school tie'. This phase is also about the rediscovery of classics like Sun Tzu's *Art of War*, Machiavelli's *The Prince* and Carl von Clausewitz's *On War*. It is still based on a military metaphor, though, and is about protecting your home turf, which was the job of the two Renaissance men depicted in Holbein's painting.

Finally, we looked at Sassetta's *The Wolf of Gubbio*, in which St Francis saves the town from a ravaging wolf by finding out what it wants and negotiating with it. The collapse of deference during the Second World War, when men and women from different social classes fought, worked and died side by side, made it much harder for leaders to assume they would be followed by default. The humanistic movement and the emergence of what we would now call Human Resources policies made followers more visible and introduced the notion that they might need to be persuaded to follow, not just ordered to do so. At the same time, women became a more noticeable part of the workforce. So leadership thinking over the last few decades in particular has been more concerned with charisma and Emotional Intelligence, the sort of skillset that might make you drop everything and follow a barefoot preacher, even if he talks to wolves rather than setting the dogs on them.

If the paintings seem a bit too highbrow, the *Wizard of Oz* works just as well. The Lion needs courage; the Scarecrow needs a brain; the Tin Man needs a heart. A good leader needs all three – and these characters also serve to represent the history of thinking about leadership.

It is almost a national sport, the perennial lists and infographics about the skills that leaders will need in the future, particularly if we are to cope with a 'VUCA' world – a world that is 'Volatile, Uncertain, Complex and Ambiguous'. It certainly feels that way. Or perhaps we are just more globally aware of it through the ubiquity of the media and the internet. While the context is changing – as it always has done – are the leaders we will need in the future so very different? I think the essence is reassuringly familiar, in the same way that parenting has changed, but remains the same. I make this claim because I started worrying about future leadership in 2003 and, in the following decade, it did not change as much as I thought. Thus, we might safely assume that these lessons will hold true for at least another decade or so. If all these think-tanks are right, we will all be on the golf course by then, while robots run our businesses, so we will not need to worry about it anyway.

So, let me set out what it is I think that leaders need to be able to do well – the basic functionality that we might programme into leader software. These are the predictable realities. If a leader gets these under their belt, it frees them up to worry about the unpredictable ones, where their leadership skills will really be tested. We will start with the idea of 20:20 foresight and how leaders learn through 'Critical Incidents'. Then we will look at the meta-competencies these teach you, before explaining all seventeen Critical Incidents in detail. For those who wish to see how these cash out, Appendix 1 lists them, with the exercises that form the second half of this book mapped against them as their constituent parts. After we have finished this chapter, we will look at the neurobiology behind them, before we move on to consider character and leadersmithing.

Future leaders

There is a story about the wizard Merlin and King Arthur in T. H. White's *The Once and Future King*. Arthur is surprised when he meets Merlin for the first time, because Merlin seems to be expecting him and has already laid the table for breakfast. Merlin explains that while normal people are born and live forwards in time, he was born at the end of time and lives life backwards. This means that he always knows what is going to happen because he has already experienced it.

It was Herman Gyr of the Stanford Research Institute who first introduced me to the writer Charles E. Smith, as part of a creativity programme that he ran for the BBC. Inspired by the story of King Arthur, Smith's 'Merlin Factor' is the leader's ability to see the potential of the present from a vantage point in the future. Smith argues that this perspective allows leaders to act in the present moment as ambassadors of a radically different future, a position that helps their organizations to achieve strategic breakthroughs, such as NASA's vision to 'put a man on the moon by the end of the decade'. I was working with a team at Ashridge, at the time, to design a programme for 'talent'. We were a bit stuck in the eternal management versus leadership loop and needed to find a way out. I loved the idea of 20:20 foresight, so we decided to define it and find out how to teach it to emerging leaders so they were job-ready for top roles. This gave rise to our now famous research question to the C-suite, way back in 2003. We asked board-level leaders: 'What do you know now as a leader that you wish you had known ten years ago?' We were surprised at how much common ground there was when we reviewed their answers. In particular, we were surprised that, unprompted, they all said they wished they had known more about themselves. When this chimed in well with the emerging literature on Emotional Intelligence, today so established, we knew we were on the right track. The other question we asked related to their hindsight wisdom: '... and how did you learn this valuable lesson?' Some of them had benefited from formal training, but the vast majority cited specific critical on-the-job incidents that had taught them what they needed to know. This resonated with something else from Arthurian lore, when Merlin teaches Arthur what it means to be a good king by turning him into different animals – a fish, a hawk, an ant, a goose and a badger. Each transformation is meant to instil a lesson which will prepare him for his future life. We asked ourselves if we could do something similar for leaders. We added together our two data sets to produce the magic potion. Then we used it to devise a simulation that provides exposure to these Critical Incidents in quite specific and realistic ways.

Critical Incidents

You will not hear anyone talking about what happens in the simulation, because past participants are sworn to secrecy to protect the learning of future participants. I can tell you that it involves a lot of actual work, several interruptions and some brilliant actors. All the detail boils down to some generics which I can share with you here. This is the full list of the Critical Incidents which our research suggests you need to master in order to feel confident at board level. I have given you the whole list of seventeen items, rather than squashing it into something more modest, so brace yourselves:

1   Stepping up
2   Taking key decisions

3   Coping with increasing change
4   Managing ambiguity
5   Taking a risk
6   Accepting when you get it wrong
7   Key board/stakeholder meeting
8   Doing the maths
9   Joining the dots
10 Motivating and influencing others
11 Flexing style
12 Delegating to and empowering staff
13 Dealing with poor performance
14 Listening to staff
15 Knowing when to seek help and advice
16 Giving and taking feedback
17 Work–life balance

The core learning objective of the simulation is about templating. It is designed to give leaders 'muscle memory' about these archetypal leadership activities, such that their bodies instinctively know how to do them. This means that when they have to perform any of these activities in their real work they feel resourced to do so. This allows leaders to meet situations head on that would normally make them feel stressed and yet still be able to maintain their cognitive functioning, because they have templates for them. This enables them not only to problem-solve well, but also to control their own response to the challenges they face.

When I was about five, my grandfather taught me how to play German Whist. In his version, the first part of the game is all about trying to win yourself the best hand by competing to win the best cards. In the second part of the game, you play for tricks. To win them, you need to have gained in the first phase the hand you need to take the game. This is essentially what building muscle memory is all about. When you train for a marathon, you build up your strength and stamina through practice runs. You never run the full 26 miles, 385 yards until the event itself, relying on your training and the adrenalin to get you through.

Over the years, the Ashridge team has simplified and grouped this list a little, for ease of use in the classroom, but the detail has stood the test of time. Of course, there is a presenting issue with using this kind of retrospective list as a guide to the future. By definition, it is using the rearview mirror to navigate. But the generic nature of the challenges that leaders have identified suggests something more perennial than I had originally thought. Perhaps these Critical Incidents function as foundational competencies and so are less susceptible to fashion. Every time I have evaluated the programme, or tailored the simulation for a new organization, I have asked their senior leaders about Critical Incidents and 'what they know now as leaders that they wish they had known ten years ago'. This means I have an extremely high level of confidence in this templating list, which has proved stable now for over a decade.

Learning pathways

If this seventeen-item list seems daunting, the research we conducted at Ashridge to assess its impact, after we had run the simulation for a few years, shows that this kind of learning rolls up into four areas of meta-learning: leadership muscle memory, self-regulation, reflective judgement and learning to learn.

1. Leadership muscle memory

By design, the simulation offers leaders the opportunity to pre-programme themselves with the behavioural templates they need for the job. Templating furnishes leaders with the muscle memory to make them resourceful, because they are able to problem-solve better under pressure. It also makes them resilient, because they know they have survived and will do so again. The confidence that comes from this type of felt experience makes leaders cautious yet fearless, which is exactly the combination they will need to get out of their own way and make the right calls in real life. Like a vaccine, the simulation infects you with small quantities of active virus, just enough to train your immune system up so that it is primed to prevent a more serious attack in the future. Through immersive templating, we are trying to give you immunity to failure. But you don't need the simulation to achieve this effect – even without it, you can still develop your own muscle memory through deliberate templating.

2. Self-regulation

Self-regulation, in cognitive terms, is the ability to calibrate your reactions and control your impulses, like avoiding calorific puddings, or not shouting at the kids. This mental capacity is at a premium for leaders because they are usually so overloaded. Any templating that you do will lessen mental load, because it stores previous solutions for reuse and adaptation, rather than them having to be built from scratch. Feeling resourced, as we shall see, allows the brain to continue to function well under pressure, multiplying this effect over time.

3. Reflective judgement

It is terribly annoying when other people are given the job you have gone for because they are more 'experienced' than you. That is why we designed this programme in the first place, for people in a hurry who do not want to sit still for the next decade, waiting to get mugged by experience in order to become more job-ready. But it remains true that in a straight fight, experience wins, because it suggests several alluring things: wisdom, measured judgement, less risk, and a knack of knowing when to panic or when just to wait. Templating helps leaders to remain cool under fire, but you also need to be famous for your discernment. Learning under pressure shows you how you react to stress and uncertainty. This helps you to face it more confidently and to see it not so much as the absence of certainty, but as an opportunity for leadership. Any idiot can slap certainty on to a situation, but premature 'solution-eering' is more populist than wise. So the aching ambiguity of our simulation – or any safe practice – provides the laboratory conditions for you to test your decision-making proclivities, before you risk applying them inappropriately in the real world. It shores up both your self-understanding and your understanding of others, so that you are not hooked by your ego into making decisions that are unwise.

4. Learning to learn

Of course there is no such thing as 20:20 foresight, unless you are Merlin. You will never be 'finished', so future-proofing your leadership means taking charge of your learning as an on-going activity. For your leadership muscles to remain supple, you need to refresh your templates and keep seeking out opportunities to acquire new ones. Exposure to a set of Critical Incidents gives you a racing start, but even in our simulation there may be some that were not attempted, or were less successful. Diarying in practice across the board is the best investment in your future potential. For any leader, our list of Critical Incidents can act as a baseline and provide an agenda for learning.

The Critical Incidents explained

So, if you wanted to use what we have learned from the simulation to build your own learning journey, what do you need to be able to do to convince yourself and others that you can lead with ease? Here are those Critical Incidents in full. These are all the things leaders told us that they wish they had nailed earlier on in their careers. If you want to cut straight to the chase, they are listed in Appendix 1 with a breakdown of their constituent templates.

1. Stepping up

Many of the leaders we spoke to had not realized that they could do the job (or not) until they got it. Maybe their boss was away or had fallen suddenly ill or they had just pulled off a stunning job interview and were now having to deliver on the rather extravagant promises made. They talked about that awful feeling when you realize, finally, that the buck stops with you. There is no one else. You have to make the decision, or take ultimate responsibility, even if the situation is not of your making. Some had been thrust into the limelight, some had sought it, but being thrown in at the deep end was widely cited as the most compelling Critical Incident of all, because it is the one when the need for you to lead is at its clearest and most public. And there is nothing that can really prepare you for it and how it will actually feel, when you are finally responsible.

The Chief Executive of one of the London boroughs told us about his first day at work. He was met at the imposing council offices by a *Downton Abbey*-style line-up and was ushered up some marble stairs to meet various dignitaries, well-wishers and staff. Eventually, he was taken to his rather grand oak-panelled office, past a long line of rather daunting-looking secretaries. We asked him what his first action was, as the new Chief Executive.

'I phoned my Mum,' he said.

So how do you practise stepping up beforehand? By finding small spheres in which you reign supreme, so you can test your mettle when the buck stops, even on something that seems minor. Stick your neck out organizing your team away day or the family holiday. Chair a committee or a task group. Deliberately draw fire, or take the blame, or stand by your decisions. All of these flex the muscles you need to build your core strength for stepping up when the day comes.

2. Taking key decisions

Along with this very final responsibility, leaders found that decision-making also feels different at the top. Organizations are typically pyramid-shaped and have a management logic. This means that the enterprise can only proceed if decisions are taken. Slow decision-making acts as a brake, freezing the organization until a decision allows it to move on. So leaders find themselves taking decisions not necessarily at a time of their own choosing, but as dictated by the needs of the organization. We know from psychological profiling that preferences vary on decision-making. Some people love making decisions and may make them too early or too hastily, because they are in a hurry to move on. Some want the best possible data before they are willing to make a call, so feel bounced and vulnerable when the organization harries them about making a decision now. In either case, bending to the needs of the organization can feel uncomfortable. But if a leader is nothing else, they are a decision-making machine – that is their function in the organizational model. Where do you sit on this continuum?

Table 1 The continuum

Shoot from the Hip	Able to Flex	Analysis Paralysis

Could you try taking decisions less frequently, or more quickly, to test your flexibility in this key domain?

3. Coping with increasing change

In evolutionary biology, there is a phenomenon called the Red Queen Effect. Named after Lewis Carroll's Red Queen, who has to run on the spot to stay in the same place, it is about the zero net gain between evolving species. Say the rabbits are getting eaten once too often. They have a meeting and decide to invest in extra sports coaching to help the youngsters outrun the foxes. This works, so the foxes get hungry and call a meeting to decide to invest in running lessons for their little foxes. The result is that both species get faster and there is no net gain.

Perhaps every generation feels this sense of having to keep running in order to stay stationary. And, if life feels like a sprint, how can you manage your team's energy – and your own – so that no one burns out? In a work culture still characterized by presenteeism, this needs serious and calculated role modelling. You could set your watch by one of my favourite bosses. In at 9.30 a.m., he always left on the dot of 5.30 p.m., every day. Only the private office knew how hard he worked on the train and in the evenings, but his actions gave everyone in the wider office permission to work normal hours, rather than feeling that they were letting the side down if they arrived after the school run or left in time for the children's bedtime. What message does your working pattern send out to your staff?

Machiavelli took the view that to keep your soldiers primed for battle, in peacetime you should pick fights to keep the troops fresh. Without exhausting your team unnecessarily, are there some small changes you can make frequently, so that they are sensitized to an environment that does not stay the same? Rearranging the office? Rotating the chairing of meetings? Different sandwiches at lunch meetings? Of course, perpetual change can feel disorientating, so finding ways to pause and regroup creates retrospective milestones and forward momentum, as well as a sense of control and manageability. In addition, apart from the small changes you make to keep things slightly in the air, what stability do you offer your colleagues? And what places of safety?

4. Managing ambiguity

Ashridge's Phil Hodgson talks about the 'ambiguity pump' in organizations. Someone junior does not know what to do, so they escalate it to their boss. The boss looks wise and says 'leave it with me'. The boss escalates it to their boss, who escalates it to their boss and so on. As the top leader, by the time you get to hear about it, a veritable tsunami of uncertainty is breaking on your desk. And you are expected to say something impressive, wise and final about the matter. One new ambassador I met was rueful about his first 100 days in post. 'Every time there was a pause in a meeting, they'd all turn to me and look expectant. So I kept filling the silence, offering opinions, solutions and decisions that I really wasn't ready for. I wish I had just kept my mouth shut. Or at least responded with a brilliant question.'

What do you do with unknowings? Do you force them into certainty, or do you let them dwell? Either way, leadersmithing is a masterclass in figuring out when to wait and when to press on.

Over the years, this need to nurse uncertainty has rejoiced under many different names. In vogue at present is the term 'negative capability', coined by the poet John Keats in a 1817 letter to his brothers, which he defined as 'that is when man is capable of being in uncertainties, mysteries, doubts, without any irritable reaching after fact & reason'. The sophomore Lewis Carroll puts something similar into the mouth of our guru the Red Queen, when she meets Alice, through the looking glass:

> Alice laughed. 'There's no use trying,' she said. 'One can't believe impossible things.'

> 'I daresay you haven't had much practice,' said the Queen. 'When I was your age, I always did it for half-an-hour a day. Why, sometimes I've believed as many as six impossible things before breakfast.'

Surfing the wave of panic that uncertainty can represent is quite a skill, but it does get easier with practice. And choosing when to act is the stuff of wisdom. The Greeks had a word for it: *kairos*. Unlike their other word for time – *chronos*, or chronological time – *kairos* is about timing. It means the right or opportune time, the 'supreme moment', when the leader has perfect timing. Can you practise hovering more consciously, waiting on the edge of knowing and learn how to feel more comfortable saying 'I don't know'?

When the UK Ministry of Defence was combining the Army, Navy and Air Force logistics arms, the lobby at the headquarters of the Quartermaster General in Andover, Hampshire, contained three large meta-plan boards about the change process. They were covered in post-it notes that could be repositioned as things changed and were the first thing staff saw as they arrived at work each morning. The first said: What We Know. The second: What We Don't Know and the third: When We Will Know. This seemed to me a brilliant way both to contain and to be honest about ambiguity and was one of the best demonstrations of change leadership I have ever seen. It also resonates with the famous Donald Rumsfeld quote about 'known unknowns'.

5. Taking a risk

So the realities of decision-making in the midst of ambiguity and in an environment of change means that it is highly likely you will be called upon to take decisions without the requisite data. Many of the leaders we talked to had stories about the exhilaration they felt when they jumped out of this metaphorical aeroplane without a parachute. For some the risk paid off and for some it did not.

The tricky thing about risk is that it is wholly relative and subjective and even the most prosaic decision can be deemed risky in retrospect if it does not work out. So this Critical Incident is a complex one. On the one hand, we heard stories about leaders taking what felt to them like a big risk, staking their very career on something; and on the other it was stories about those calculated risks that make other people panic but actually feel quite safe to you. So this is partly about the 'feel the fear and do it anyway' element and partly about mopping up afterwards. You would be suspicious if you met a child without scabs on their knees. These are their badges of honour for taking risks and learning from them. What risks have you taken in your life? What did you learn from them? What risks did you avoid taking and can you learn from them too?

6. Accepting when you get it wrong

Statistically speaking, then, you will make some mistakes. Even with the best intentions and the best data, facts change, unforeseen conse-quences arise, or history is a harsh judge. It is 'your fault' yet it is not. This is where the pain of leadership is felt most keenly. The market moves, staff are let go; marriages may break up and lives collapse. Then the market moves back and they need not have lost their jobs after all, but it is too late to repair the damage done. How do you bear guilt for your part in misery, even if it was never part of your plan to cause it? Globally, there are a host of ex-world leaders expiating for the sins of office by pursuing world peace and through charity work. Some leaders deal with this by internalizing the pain and tend to suffer acute stress and heart disease as a result – heart-broken indeed. Not for nothing do we wince at the 'before and after' photographs of Tony Blair and Barack Obama, with their tired faces and grey hair. Others deal with it through partition, by divorcing themselves from their role. This tends to show up in an increasingly robotic boss who seems to have hollow eyes and no soul. By far the hardest path is to sit with the pain and try to forgive yourself for it. Blessed are those leaders who have a wisdom tradition or spiritual practice to help them at this point. Any mistake made needs to be owned. You may or may not want to admit publicly to the mistake. Some need to be borne bravely and in secret. Others need to be domesticated through socialization so they cannot hurt anyone any more. But you need to be able to sleep at night. If you cannot, your ability to make better decisions next time will be eroded, because you need sleep to bank the day's data in your memory. If you do not do so, the database will become increasingly dated and empty and your ability to make good decisions will reduce, as will your health, without the opportunity for night-time repair that is afforded by deep sleep. But do not delude yourself, you will need a confessional. So find one early, before you really need it. It might be a person, a practice or a ritual, but you need somewhere to go for purification, to keep your leading healthy and your followers safe from you.

7. Key board/stakeholder meetings

Many of the leaders we spoke to had come a cropper at a key meeting. A technical disaster, an unexpected question, hostile shareholders, or a board who have suddenly lost confidence in you. This was one of the Critical Incidents where people had learned the hard way, making them usefully paranoid about future meetings and presentations and more aware of the need for rehearsal and scenario planning to guard against blind spots. What do you do to prepare for set pieces? If you still think it is somehow cool to wing it, sack yourself now. Your organization does not need saboteurs. You owe it to them to practise and to get feedback, no matter how tedious it feels. You may think you can control yourself and your technology, but you may not be able to control your audience, so gaming likely questions or blind spots will repay all the time you put in. If not this time, then sometime, because those challenges can come at you from any side in any context, so being ready is simply wise. And there is no shame in seeking out training, coaching and help. Remember, in ancient Rome, rhetoric was the sole preoccupation of the gentleman scholar. Today we are in danger of forgetting this art, because we can wow the crowds with technology. But its power remains, with the speeches and TED talks that go viral reminding us that the basics of human connection and storytelling do not change much over time.

8. Doing the maths

One of the crunchier Critical Incidents revealed by our research concerns finance. I have always been struck by how diligently the Foreign & Commonwealth Office prepares its staff for a posting abroad. In particular, it takes language training very seriously. And the language of business is finance. Converting activity into numbers allows those managing the enterprise or concerned with its performance to track progress and to compare different activities. So why do we let some leaders claim that numbers are not their thing? It is rude to live in France and have no French and it makes it hard to operate like a native there.

If you do not know the language of numbers, you had better start learning it now. Otherwise you lay yourself open to the risk of taking decisions in the dark, in an environment where decision-making is already a risky business. This was a Critical Incident where leaders gloried in an ability to explain the business to itself, through the language of numbers and by articulating strategy and priorities. For many, the penny dropped when they finally found a story that said it all for them.

One leader of a professional services firm I worked for had a story about 'throwing in the taps'. In its analysis, the firm had discovered that in order to win pitches, partners had been adding in all kinds of extras which rendered the margin on the work minimal. So when the leader delivered a speech to the whole organization about the need to tighten belts, he told a funny story about a plumber who was forever 'throwing in the taps' to sweeten the deal with clients. It turned out that the brass taps cost more than the ceramic basins they adorned, so his largesse was putting him out of business. This simple analogy had the whole firm talking about 'brass taps' and starting to pay much closer attention both to hidden costs and to the pricing of individual elements within their pitch documents.

9. Joining the dots

How well can you join the dots across your organization? Old-fashioned organizations often encouraged breadth and career paths criss-crossed internal boundaries. Many organizations today hire experts instead. So, unless you have an MBA – or a gym or a smoking room – many of today's leaders will have less of a handle on the detail of how other departments work and how the pieces of the organizational jigsaw fit together. And a lack of understanding contributes to silo mentalities, fiefdoms and narrowly competitive behaviour. You may have played the game where a 'newspaper' has been torn up. Each of you has a number of random pieces. You have to put your section back together so that the paper can 'go to press' on time. Cue lots of hoarding of pieces and devious negotiating strategies. Of course, this is a trick. The proper thing to do is for everyone to lay their pieces down and do the task together, because you all work for the newspaper and want it to succeed. Don't feed a silo mentality. If any part of your organization is a mystery to you, go and spend a day there.

One of the ice-breakers I use in large conferences is to ask each table of delegates to come up with something they all have in common. This can seem a tall order, if they cannot use the default of 'attending the same event today'. But eventually we uncover stories about second languages or holidays; similar pets or children; or where they bought their beds or their underwear. Difference can be distracting, but there is always commonality hidden beneath, if we search for it. And inhabiting strange worlds is the best way to learn what is really different and what is really the same, as well as how everything contributes to the whole. Investing your time here will tool you up both for understanding difference better and for being able to appeal to superordinate goals when you need to get things done in the future.

10. Motivating and influencing others

Oh dear. You have made it to the top and somehow you thought you would be in charge once you got there. You would have control over people and they would do what you say. But when you are finally there, you know as you never really knew before that you can only deliver through others. And what if they do not want to, or do not know how to, or do not understand? Heaven forfend that you should think the bullying approach of Sugar or Trump in *The Apprentice* is an effective way to proceed. There are myriad ways you can address this challenge. The best I have found is to use the Gallup 12 as your scorecard and to keep working on it like a fanatic until you score a perfect twelve from all of your colleagues.

The Gallup 12 is a famous study that was launched under the strapline 'people leave managers not companies'. In 1999, Marcus Buckingham and Curt Coffman published their write-up of two large Gallup surveys undertaken over a twenty-five-year period, involving over 1 million employees and 80,000 managers from a broad range of companies, industries and countries. Their study identified twelve questions that measured the strength of a workplace, which were tested on a sample of over 105,000 employees from 2,500 business units across twenty-four companies, to find out whether, in practice, a strong workplace would equate to a more profitable workplace. The following twelve questions, when answered positively, correlated with higher levels of productivity, profit, retention and customer satisfaction:

1 Do you know what is expected of you at work?
2 Do you have the materials and equipment you need to do your work right?
3 At work, do you have the opportunity to do what you do best every day?
4 In the last seven days, have you received recognition or praise for doing good work?
5 Does your supervisor, or someone at work, seem to care about you as a person?
6 Is there someone at work who encourages your development?
7 At work, do your opinions seem to count?
8 Does the purpose of your organization make you feel your job is important?
9 Are your colleagues committed to doing quality work?
10 Do you have a best friend at work?
11 In the last six months, has someone at work talked to you about your progress?
12 In the last year, have you had opportunities at work to learn and grow?

Most of the twelve questions essentially boil down to whether or not a manager shows an interest in staff and provides them with regular support and feedback. What was new about these findings was how overwhelmingly they suggested that employee satisfaction drives business performance. A version of the twelve questions is now used in many organizations both to predict, track and compare monthly earnings across different stores or sites and through pulse surveys. But the research also means that the single most important influence on an organization's performance is the manager. The hard message from this research is that if your team are not performing, it is probably your fault.

11. Flexing style

Joy is a good word for how it feels, when you have been stuck in an infinite loop with a staff member, trying harder and harder, when suddenly – usually through exasperation – you try something different. And at that shift in approach, suddenly the lights come on. They seem to wake up, 'get it' and are galvanized into action. Abraham Maslow once said that if the only tool you have is a hammer, everything looks like a nail. This Critical Incident is about weaning you off any style habits you may have developed, in case an over-reliance on them is restricting your ability to get the best out of those around you.

One of the kinaesthetic exercises we use at Ashridge to talk about style is a 'ballroom dancing' challenge. In pairs, palm to palm and in silence, couples have to navigate round the room, avoiding bumping into the other couples doing the same. In the first iteration, the leader 'pushes' his partner around the room. Provided the partner does not dig their heels in and refuse to move, this feels pretty straightforward. The leader can see the way ahead and protects their partner from harm by piloting them carefully around the other couples. Then we swap and the leader tries this time to 'pull' their partner around the room, again palm to palm and avoiding the other couples around them. This time the leader cannot see where they are going and has to rely on their partner to keep with them, for if the palm-to-palm contact is broken they are no longer leading. When we debrief this, groups are usually split fairly evenly between a preference for pushing and one for pulling. We talk about the circumstances in which each of the styles would be most appropriately used and when one might need to override natural preferences to deploy the best style for the task in hand. Then we ask about how it felt to be led in this exercise. While some people will admit to finding being pushed quite relaxing ('I just closed my eyes') the majority always prefer being pulled to being pushed, because they feel a sense of partnership and responsibility and they can see where they are going. This resonates with all staff surveys ever, in which junior staff invariably feel under-used, under-trusted and under-acknowledged and just want the opportunity to prove themselves through more interesting work.

The Emotional Intelligence guru Daniel Goleman's famous 'golf clubs' metaphor on style breaks the push-and-pull styles down with more granularity. His Push styles are Coercive, Authoritative and Pace-setting. He recommends the coercive style ('do what I say') for emergencies, turnarounds and when working with problem employees. But overuse of it will inhibit organizational flexibility and dampen employee motivation. His authoritative style ('come with me') works well when a business is adrift, but will not work when your followers are more expert than you are. His pace-setting style ('do as I do, now') sets high standards and role-models them, which works well with employees who are highly competent and self-motivated. But it can feel relentless and overwhelming for those who struggle.

Goleman's Pull styles are Affiliative, Democratic and Coaching. He recommends the affiliative style ('people come first') to build harmony in a team or to increase morale, but overuse can allow poor performance go unchallenged. The democratic style ('what do you think?') works well to build a sense of participation and to generate new ideas, but overuse results in endless meetings and a lack of momentum. The coaching style ('try this') focuses more on personal development, so it works well with staff who want to improve. It could well backfire, however, and feel like coercion in sheep's clothing, to an employee who does not see the need for change and is resistant to it. As in a game of golf, you would not putt with a driver, or drive with a putter. To play a perfect round you carefully select the club you need for the shot you want to play. So a good leader can handle all the clubs well and interchanges them with ease.

Sometimes, though, it is less about style and more about being locked in a pattern. There is an interesting book called *Change* by Paul Watzlawick, John Weakland and Richard Fisch, in which they explain the concept of 'stuck patterns' in human relating. Have you ever tried the nine-dot puzzle? You have to join all the dots with four straight lines without lifting the pen.

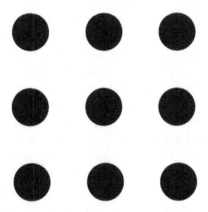

Figure 2 The nine-dot puzzle

It is very annoying when you see how it is done (see Appendix 2). It can only be solved by 'thinking outside the box' because, as Einstein famously said, we cannot solve problems by using the same kind of thinking we used when we created them. Watzlawick applies this logic to people.

Do you ever feel like you are stuck in a time warp with someone, where the same conversation just keeps happening, on an infinite loop? They argue that we get so fixated on 'changing the other person' that we neglect our own role in keeping the pattern going. It goes a bit like this. A report keeps coming in riddled with errors which have to be corrected before it can go out. You decide to tackle the problem by sitting down with your colleague to coach them through the process, by being clear about what you want. But because you want to have time to check it properly next time, you agree an earlier deadline. The next time the report arrives, it is worse. Why? Because your colleague has had less time to devote to it and knew you would check it anyway. So you repeat the process, you 'try harder' to get your colleague to smarten up. And so it continues, because the solution has now become the problem. You are getting increasingly wound-up and putting a lot of energy into the process, but your colleague seems to you to be making less and less effort.

This is like the First Law of Thermodynamics. The amount of energy in the system seems to be constant, but now rather than it being your colleague who is expending great energy writing accurate reports, you are expending great energy fixing them. Those of you with the messy teenage bedroom problem will be used to experiencing a similar sense of disproportion. Watzlawick reasonably asks, why not just let go? If you stop sustaining the 'stuckness' with your energy, the pattern cannot hold. Say you let your colleague know that they can send the report straight out in future. Might they not check diligently this time? Or at least truly understand your point of view if it is badly received? Of course, you have to manage the risk of letting go, but noticing you are in a stuck pattern is the first step towards identifying 'out of the box' solutions. My favourite lesson from the Watzlawick book? A cure for insomnia. Instead of screwing your eyes shut and counting sheep, just try to keep your eyes open. You will get so bored staring at nothing you will soon fall asleep.

12. Delegating to and empowering staff

One leader we interviewed said a very wise thing about delegation and choosing what work to do. It is his 'lead through/learn from' criterion. Essentially, leaders should not 'do' anything: as a guiding principle, they should delegate it all, so they are free to 'lead'. The exceptions to this rule are those tasks through which the leader can be seen to be leading, or those from which they can learn. Too often we do the tasks we like or are good at, or the ones that feel important or that others want us to do. This rule suggests that we should only do the tasks we find it hardest to do so that we might learn from them. After all, supple learning muscles are your first line of defence in a VUCA environment. The other set of tasks we should do are those that provide opportunities for us to lead. These tasks might be stacking shelves, taking a media interview, phoning a customer or visiting a site – all things that are delegatable, but which can also become mouthpieces for culture.

Leaders lead through stories and through the personal touch, and I think leaders are like lighthouses: the ships they save rarely come close, but all are led by their light or abandoned by their darkness.

13. Dealing with poor performance

Our research found that most leaders avoid difficult conversations because they are terrified either of making women cry or men shout. They do not want to be the bad guy and they do not want to get it wrong and end up in court. Well, have you ever given any thought to what baby zebras learn at nursery? I would imagine they are taught how to run away from predators. But I will bet there is something else they learn. That you need not be the fastest zebra – indeed breaking away from the pack has its own risks – you just need to be faster than the slowest zebra. Because the lion can only eat one at a time. And while he is munching the hindquarters of your unfortunate colleague, you can escape. I think this happens in organizations, too. While the boss is going on difficult conversations courses to avoid having one and spending hours off with a coach worrying about it, everyone else clocks that the focus is on Slow Joe, so they ease their foot off the accelerator. Over time, performance across the board starts to dip, because clearly the boss does not care enough about quality to actually pull Joe up for it, so why bother? If you ever thought that it was just about you and Joe, think again. What is at stake here is the performance of your entire team. Put this book down and go and talk to Joe now. Do it for them.

14. Listening to staff

When Gary Hamel pillories Michael Porter's approach to strategy in their popular gladiatorial bouts, he likes to say of organizations that 'the bottleneck is at the top of the bottle'. His view is that the very experience that has got executives to the top of their organizations is now irrelevant and even dangerous. These people should not be trusted with strategy, which is about a future their past will make it hard for them to see. He thinks that the staff at the bottom of the organization are often the ones who have access to the authentic customer experience. They handle complaints, they empty bins, they overhear conversations in lifts, cars and lobbies. That is why so many leaders guard their PAs and drivers so jealously – they are a hotline to the pulse of the organization. And even the most zealous of change agents will admit that resistance can sometimes be useful. Sometimes staff resist change because they know something you do not know. They know it will not work and why. But you preferred to hire in those top-flight strategy consultants who had industry benchmarks, to save you distracting staff by gathering your own. Resistance is data. Complaints are feedback. And exit interviews? You should be handling those yourself. Knowing why they leave and where they go tells you all you need to know about who is winning the war for talent. In one company I worked for, HR flagged CVs from staff working for competitors, so we could keep tabs not just on things like pay, but also on new software projects, clients or markets. So please do not be like the leader we spoke to who made an embarrassing public mistake, only to find out later that a timely warning from a junior member of staff had been blocked by a well-meaning courtier who did not want to rain on his boss's parade.

Art Kleiner's Core Group Theory explains why leaders are particularly vulnerable to incomplete information. Essentially, Kleiner argues that the core group in any organization has the same effect as does a magnet on iron filings. When they are around, everyone snaps to attention. I see it visibly when we have certain CEOs or Ministers come in to address a course: the fanning out, the standing up straight, the self-conscious gesturing, the laughing at their jokes, the sounding slightly better-spoken than usual and, of course, the asking of terribly clever questions. Kleiner suggests there are a couple of phenomena at play here which can be very powerful and potentially dangerous. One is the power of *attention*. Whatever they see you looking at will get their attention, too. When I was at Deloitte, we had a new MD. His first act was to phone up every single person who had submitted their timesheet late that week. It did not happen again.

This gaze shades into another phenomenon – *follow-my-leader*. One trivial example is a CEO I interviewed, who had received cufflinks for Christmas. Not wanting to upset his kind wife, he had invested in double-cuff shirts so he could wear them. To his horror, by the end of the month he noticed that all of his senior team had started wearing cufflinks, too.

The third phenomenon is that of *amplification*, or distortion. This might be a bad commute and a bad temper in the office which, by lunchtime, the grapevine has translated into job losses and financial collapse. Or it could be an off-the-cuff remark or the accidental encouraging of bad behaviour through benign neglect or a wish not to be unpopular. Facebook's COO Sheryl Sandberg is rueful about a 'No PowerPoint' rule she once announced for her meetings in the United States. A few weeks later, she was told that 'Europe' were upset with her, because they found pitching to clients without PowerPoint rather hard. So she had to explain to the entire global sales team that she had just been expressing a personal preference for local meetings with her, not an absolute global company rule.

Kleiner suggests that we will always try to please our core group and, in the absence of data, we will create the facts and facsimiles we need to be loyal regents. The Japanese have a particular emotion to describe this 'pleasurable sense of dependence', which translates as *amae*. This basking in being parented may stop followers from wanting to break this dependence, either by behaving like an adult or peer, or by doing anything that might attract the leader's displeasure. This makes it likely that those closest to you may only tell you what they think you want to hear. Make sure you are clear that they risk your displeasure by not telling you things and hedge this risk by making sure your informal channels – that famous driver or PA – are also available to you, too. And, could your youngest recruit become your upward mentor? Harvest the first impressions of your new staff, before they stop noticing what is around them.

15. Knowing when to seek help and advice

This Critical Incident stands witness to all those leaders who were too proud to admit they might not have all the answers already. All those years of being fed heroic leaders as role models takes its toll. Because of the relentless ambiguity of leading, no one will ever truly know what to do, but followers tend to demand certainty when times are tough and it feels a betrayal not to offer it to them. Be careful about how you get help and who you use, because the act is not a neutral one and the message it sends out can be unhelpful. We all know leaders who have lost respect because of their over-reliance on a manipulative lieutenant or coach or who waste fortunes on the wrong consultants in a bid to shore up their authority. But finding a trusted 'kitchen cabinet' is the chief task of any great leader. So do not be a hero if it is not wise to fly solo, but be canny about the politics of taking advice.

16. Giving and taking feedback

In our original research, this Critical Incident started being about dealing with praise, whether from a boss, peers or more junior staff. Perhaps it is just a British thing, to find praise so chronically uncomfortable. Learning to say 'thank you' with grace, instead of belittling the feedback (and, thereby, its messenger), seems hard to master. In our focus group discussions, this quickly widened out into a more general conversation about key moments when feedback had been transformational. It remains true that senior people often do not get good quality feedback, because their position tends to invite either invective or sycophancy. Neither are developmental in character. So when someone had bothered to deliver hard messages well or to honour strengths in a specific way, our leaders had felt exhilarated and galvanized into bestowing the same favour on colleagues in future. Often a blind spot had held them back, or a lack of confidence, and the energy this released boosted their leadership career. And it does not much matter which feedback model you use, it just matters that you give feedback and give it well.

Taking harsh feedback, on the other hand, can be painful, but it comes with the territory. It is what academics Peter Frost and Sandra Robinson would call 'toxic handling'. This is learning how to take hurtful and destructive feedback, because you are the leader and it is your job to absorb it and to earth it like a lightning conductor, so that it cannot do any more harm to the organization. Learning to welcome opportunities to bear pain for the organization, but to protect yourself from taking this too personally, requires both strength and wisdom. In too many instances it just causes stress and conflict. The leaders we spoke to wished they had known at the time that it was not personal, it was just the job and that the gift of providing this service to the organization was the best possible way they could have led it through hard times.

17. Work–life balance

Oscar Wilde wrote a heart-rending fairy tale called *The Happy Prince* (1888). In it, a swallow befriends the statue of a town's late prince. From his plinth, the Happy Prince sees his people suffering and asks the swallow to help them, using the decoration from his statue. The ruby is taken from his sword hilt, the sapphires are plucked from his eyes and the gold leaf covering his body is torn off by the swallow, to alleviate the plight of the poor. The Mayor walks by and looks up. Seeing the now ugly statue, he orders it to be pulled down and thrown away.

This story is a great parable for all those people who give of themselves too much. The Clore Social Leadership Programme has a great model: Know Yourself, Be Yourself, Look After Yourself. Particularly in the social sector, it is tempting to think that you are virtuous if you work hard and work late and are deeply heroic in your job performance. But what happens to your organization if you simply use yourself up?

I have worked with some clergy who think that their job is to use themselves up in service of others. It has even got a fancy theological name – '*kenosis*', or self-emptying. But I think this is a confusion and, at its worst, it has a lot more to do with ego than with selflessness. Yes, you are special and unique, but other people are also special and unique and are also called to serve, whether in the religious life, through volunteering, or through their work or caring. What more could you do, not only to set an example about work-life balance to those whom you lead, but also to grow talent around you and share the work around? In a country where 21 per cent of 18–24 year-olds are unemployed, our culture of overworking is having devastating consequences. Senior people are burning out from overwork, while there is an acute shortage of jobs for entry-level candidates.

And the business case? Overworking causes stress, which has a negative effect on your ability to sleep well. If you do not get good quality sleep, your ability to form memories and make good decisions will diminish. You, therefore, become a risk to your organization because you cannot remember things. You also become more prone to lose control, which makes your behaviour less predictable, rendering you a less reliable colleague overall.

However, even if you overcome all of that and keep working hard, be careful. Do check that the career ladder you are climbing is up against the right wall. It would be a shame to make it right to the top, only to see lots of other ladders you now realize you prefer.

These seventeen Critical Incidents, then, are the master list that we distilled from our research. This is our best guess about what it is that leaders need to be able to do to lead well. If any of them would keep you awake at night, or stop you applying for your next role, you can go ahead and schedule them in now. You can use Appendix 1 to help you. If you can learn how to do all seventeen well, you will have nothing to fear. But how do you take a long list like this and turn it into a magic potion for leaders-in-waiting? Answering that question made us look again at everything we know about how leaders really learn.

Chapter 2

How Do Leaders Really Learn?

Designed to work

Now we know what it is that leaders need to be able to do well, what is the best way to teach it to them? Answering this question requires a quick primer on how the brain works before we move on. This chapter will set out the research base for a leadersmithing approach to learning, so feel free to skip it if theory is not your thing.

When we designed the Future Leaders programme at Ashridge, Emotional Intelligence was just making its debut as a standard component on leadership programmes. I had started teaching it to clients like the Ministry of Defence and became increasingly interested in its account of the brain. I now have a plastic model of a brain that I take with me when I am teaching. It has all kinds of intriguing labels, for things like the medulla oblongata and the corpus callosum. But I think the whole brain thing can really be explained pretty simply. Neurobiologists or those of a purist nature look away now ...

Let us look at the species that holds the record for survival: reptiles. OK, maybe bacteria wins on points, but we will use crocodiles as our case study, because of our biological similarity. So, when we were all being crocodiles, how clever were we? Pretty good at dozing in the mud. Pretty good at shooting out to catch prey. Pretty great at surviving. But take one to a chick flick ...? We even joke about their lack of emotional intelligence – 'crocodile tears' is the most cynical of charges. So thumbs up for survival; thumbs down for neural complexity. But we evolved. Became mammalian. Bigger brains that added bits on to deal with all that nuance. Elephants grieving. Dogs peeing in your shoe. Cats sulking while you are away. There is even a whole movie about a weeping camel. Mammals got good at emotion. Then came Homo Erectus; then Homo Sapiens. Now we can get deeply complex about nested emotions, with Shakespeare's Juliet exclaiming 'My only love sprung from my only hate!' You can get degrees in this stuff. But if you look at my plastic brain, with its familiar pickled walnut exterior, you will notice that there is another sort of nut hidden deep in its interior. The amygdala, named after the Greek word for 'almond'. This is the vestige of our reptilian brain. Why did we keep it? Because reptiles are the experts on survival. This suggests that we need to pay careful attention to the things that the almond does for us.

Say a child runs up to give you a drawing. Your brain registers the event, a bit like you taking a photograph of it on your phone. In order to drive out a response to the event, your brain sends this picture into Filing Central. They do a quick reconciliation, find a match and brief a response: hunker down, accept the picture and offer fulsome praise about the colour or energy of the piece, even if you have no clue what it is supposed to be. And when your body is in a state of physiological calm, this is exactly how the process works: data in, matching process, reaction out.

We have that almond bit of our brain, too. In deference to its status as the guardian of our longevity, Filing Central sends a courtesy copy of the data to your amygdala. But like many of the emails you are cc'd into, to the amygdala most of this looks like junk. Imagine your amygdala is a bit like the worst kind of stereotypical teenager, compared with Dr Oxbridge in Filing Central, who has a PhD in filing and is massively thorough and diligent. He has kept meticulous records of every-thing that has ever happened to you. His system is extraordinary, but pretty full, so sometimes it takes a while to find things. Contrast your teenager, who only does Cool. So old stuff, repeat stuff? Straight in the bin. He only keeps big news. Like the day your childhood was ruined by the arrival of that younger sibling. Or when Santa Got It Wrong. Your first bike. Your first school. Your first kiss. If we were to study his photo album of memories, it would look a bit faded, dated and sepia, with 80s' shoulder-pads and haircuts and lots of early pictures that peter out into the occasional high-octane record of a birth, or a marriage, or a death. Comparing these two filing systems is salutary. Ordinarily the risk represented by the patchiness of the amygdala's data set is contained, because Dr Oxbridge is in charge. But beware – your amygdala's job is the survival of the species, so he takes precedence if you are ever in peril. When your body perceives a threat, the amygdala seizes control from your rational brain. And he is able to react more quickly, because he has much less data to wade through before he finds you an answer.

We need to pay careful attention to his strengths and limits, however. Here is an example. Imagine yours truly being fabulous when she worked for Deloitte. One day, a client discovered an error in an email. He went bananas. Everyone he rang to complain was out, so eventually he rang me. He shouted a lot and used words down the phone that I had better not put in this book. And my reaction? I wanted to go to the loo. Not the most career-enhancing move. And perhaps 'evacuation' is just a normal stress response. But when I thought more about it, it made me wonder. The shouting had made me feel threatened. Poole in peril! My amygdala had rushed out to save me. It had scoured the photo album for precedents and found a match: ranting senior male person? My dad; me, aged three; accused of causing a jam jar to fall and smash an ancestral fruit bowl. And what is a particularly brilliant reaction when you are 3? Yes! An 'accident' – your dad will soon head back indoors to fetch your mum to cope with the bathroom admin. So the shouting stops. Age 30? Not such a smart response.

But what was my amygdala up to? One, he was trying to buy me time – make the shouty man stop. Two, he was trying to get a message out to me: this is not your fault. On both occasions I had been wrongly accused, but the shouting needed to stop before I could make my argument. What I also learned from this was how empty my filing cabinet was. My amygdala had not been able to find anything other than this rather retro 1975 template for 'shouty man'. So I got busy. For the next year I embarked on a range of minor 'picking fights' experiments, until I had a whole range of templates to help me in times of conflict. Indeed, a year later I had a repeat experience, when a fuming male colleague rang to shout at me about something. This time, I noticed with delight that all this templating now enabled me to stand tall and have a grown-up conversation with him, rather than having to exit stage left to the nearest loo.

Remember, your amygdala is trying to keep you safe and will be generating data. That funny feeling when the phone rings? Not you being silly, but an extremely sophisticated sixth sense designed to protect you from danger. And if sometimes it gets it wrong, that is more to do with an incomplete data set than a poor intention. If you have any areas of vulnerability in relation to your reactions, do not accept it, schedule in the acquisition of fresh templates. Garbage in, garbage out – you are only as good as the resources you have to draw on in times of trouble.

It was this basic insight that informed the 'muscle memory' design and the idea of templating. But, with the advent of more sophisticated accounts of leadership learning and the brain, was this learning working the way we thought it was? We set about addressing this question in a variety of ways.

Impact assessment

The Ashridge simulation was designed from theory, so we were anxious from the outset to test outcomes against the design. Over the years, we conducted a series of evaluations of the simulation. The first one was led by Megan Reitz, where we asked a cross-section of alumni whether the 'muscle memory' we had helped them create had proved useful. Our findings can be summarized by this account:

> I really do think that the difficult conversation practice has given me an awareness of what pressure situations will do to me. When I'm in a situation where I'm really feeling uncomfortable I will start drawing my breath, I will start going red and feeling a bit tight about the person and noticing my pitch and tone of voice. As soon as I start feeling that now, I know that I'm going to go. But now I have the understanding to say 'hang on a minute, do you mind if I just grab a glass a water?' and stop myself. It's that kind of self-awareness that is really invaluable for me, because it means I'm now in control of myself.

This is exactly what we wanted. The ability to experience a situation and be better resourced to deal with it. And to have the thinking time to make that call. And this learning process is very transferable.

Vertical development

As well as this ability to 'do' leadership better under pressure, we became curious about what the process was teaching participants about the nature of leadership itself. Professor Kurt Fischer from the Harvard Graduate School of Education came over to help us with this, based on his idea of 'dynamic skill theory', which our colleague Ellen Pruyne studied with him for her PhD. Fischer belongs to a school of theory which holds that the more you learn about something, the more complex your understanding of it becomes. This is why learning in a messy way is so vital.

Fischer's colleague Theo Dawson calls this process 'Vertical Development'. We know that senior leaders, by definition, need to be able to handle a wider range of perspectives, cope with more ambiguity and continue to make wise decisions in spite of uncertainty. We also know that learning involves both the accumulation of knowledge and the organizing of that knowledge into mental maps. As we develop, our mental maps become increasingly complex and this complexity in turn allows for more complex thinking. This increasing capacity to handle complexity is Vertical Development. Dawson developed a Lectical Assessment System to measure it and has used it in a variety of organizations to show that this ability to think complexly increases with seniority. This suggests either that senior people are picked for this ability, or that they naturally develop it during their career. Her findings also suggest that many senior roles demand higher levels of Vertical Development than the post-holders are able to display. High levels of Vertical Development would give you leaders who are better able to solve complex problems, which suggests an approach to development and talent planning that is less about answers than about reasoning ability and the use of good questions.

Fischer liked our programme, because he had not found any other approach to leadership development that had been able to get this complexity across. Most approaches tend to reduce leadership to simple definitions and models for ease of teaching and to reduce the learner's cognitive load. But this simplicity does leadership a particular disservice, by making it appear too simple. What the Harvard evaluation showed us was that learning through experience, particularly under pressure, gives leaders a usefully nuanced understanding of what leading means, as well as a felt sense of how complex and messy it really is.

Neurobiological assessment

Knowing how effective the learning was, we wanted to learn whether or not we could fine-tune our approach. Exactly how was it working, which bits and why? So we teamed up with Professor Patricia Riddell from the University of Reading to apply insights from neurobiology to the process.

We started with a snippet of theory about stress. All performers know the benefits of first night butterflies, that surge of adrenaline when you are primed and ready to go. The idea behind the 'fight-or-flight' stress response is that our brains are conditioned to work best when we are in 'fight' mode, to give us the best chance of survival. Once we are in 'flight' mode, we need less complex cognitive functioning and more physical prowess, so our bodies reprioritize for us. The Harvard team of Kassam, Koslov and Mendes have explained that this is less of an absolute decision and more of a psychological one. We will stay in 'fight' mode for as long as we believe that we have the personal resources to prevail. Being resourced to cope is not a scientific measure, it is a feeling, an instantaneous decision we make, which is why you hear stories about 'hysterical strength', when grannies lift cars off toddlers when they should not have been able to. And because these fight-or-flight states can be measured by monitoring changes in cardiovascular efficiency, we were able to use heart monitors to gauge how the leaders in our simulation were dealing with the Critical Incidents they faced.

Using psychometrics, questionnaires, heart monitors, video-recording and observational data, we discovered that the simulation both accelerates learning and extends the shelf-life of that learning by embedding it deep in the emotional memory. You learn faster and you acquire memories that last. Specifically, increased heart rate during the simulation was correlated with higher levels of learning, which remained high throughout the period of post-programme testing. We also found that the learning was largely independent of any demographic or psychometric variation between participants and did not vary by gender.

And the good news is that 'feeling resourced to cope' is very easy to manipulate. We just have to spot where you do not feel resourced and take you through a process that makes you feel better, like practising difficult conversations until you are not scared of them any more. Because of how your body works, it so happens that learning under pressure is quicker than normal learning. This is because pressure primes your brain to optimize its performance, because it might be a matter of life and death. Even without pressure, raised heart rate has been shown to accelerate brain functioning, but we are also after the shelf-life and retrievability of your learning, which is where memory-tagging comes in. Learning obtained under pressure gets tagged as being useful for future survival, so it gets stored in your memory emotionally, as well as cognitively, which flags it as a priority memory and makes it retrievable under pressure, as well as in situations of calm.

One of the best things about learning under pressure is that it helps you to identify your 'stretch zone' thresholds. Figuring out where your 'fight' mode is matters because it is where you will be at your cognitive best. Like the top performers in sport and the arts, you need to be able to step into this space when it really counts. It is not healthy to stay there for long, but it is where your brain is at its keenest. And now we know that if you can spot where you are under-resourced, you can keep extending this high-performing space, by systematically resourcing yourself to cope.

How might you do that, exactly? Here is a worked example of a common leadership competence, about an ability to hold your own at board level in the C-suite. This is mainly about being perceived to be an authority, but is also about adding value across the business as a whole in co-leading it. In our Critical Incidents' list (see Chapter 1), this would be about equipping yourself to handle key board/stakeholder meetings well. Baby steps might involve limbering up with a subscription to an industry journal or the *Harvard Business Review*. Perhaps you might set up a Twitter feed to follow key figures in your sector to see what is on their minds. You might also acclimatize by availing yourself of free on-line modules, TED talks, podcasts and talking books to fill in any gaps in your understanding about the business. These are all below the radar. Next, you might edge out into common view by refreshing your impact and presentation skills through training. You might also set up some job shadowing of key leaders, customers, suppliers or partners, or spend time shadowing business units whose work is unfamiliar to you. To raise the stakes a bit, you could arrange to present back your findings at a team meeting or write a blog or article on lessons learned. This might start raising your heart rate, which should help cement the learning. You could capitalize on these experiences by taking on a formal MBA-style training course or refresher, again with reporting-back routines built in, or you could seek out a secondment to a key partner or in another region. If you want to build your profile further within your industry, you could then publish a Point of View in a key industry magazine or guest lecture on an MBA course. Ultimately, you could register to deliver a keynote at an industry conference and offer mentoring and masterclasses in your field to other staff and key contacts.

These examples show a slowly slowly approach that builds confidence and resourcefulness at each stage. The higher the stakes the better, provided you manage the risk well, so you may wish just to dive in at one of the harder levels. That is where the stickiest learning will occur, but the lower rungs of the ladder might help you to feel less exposed when you get there.

Mechanical heart rate

Can you just raise your heart rate mechanically, while reading a book on leadership, and get the same benefits? Well, to a degree. One of our colleagues at the University of Reading set about answering this question. For her MSc, Kathryn Breheny persuaded twenty postgraduate students to participate in a study involving exercise bikes to measure the impact of exercise on reading and comprehension. The study showed that reading speed and comprehension increased after ten minutes of cycling. Great news if you need to focus your attention to plough through a tedious report! This study supports associated research into links between exercise, or the mechanical increase in heart rate, and cognitive functioning, which will tend to improve both during and directly after the heart rate has been raised. The explanation usually given is that, as hunter–gatherers, the brain optimizing in motion was a vital part of our ability to survive, literally problem-solving on the hoof as we avoided threats and searched out sustenance.

However, while this would help with the acquisition of memories, because the brain has a sharper experience when heart rate is raised, it is another thing to be able to retrieve the memories again subsequently.

Where learning under pressure seems to trump its mechanical cousin is in this vital arena. Thinking about the mammalian brain's Dr Oxbridge, who we have met before, imagine that quality time in the gym makes him much nippier racing around his library filing memories, ever more beautifully recorded in calligraphy on pristine index cards. Sure, he is up to date and his system is optimized, but his gold-standard processes still get over-ridden under pressure when the amygdala pulls rank. This means that, as well as any exercise-induced optimization, a leader will be best protected for the future if they have also populated their amygdala with a memory of any Critical Incident experienced. As we know from the work of academics like Elizabeth Phelps and Tony Buchanan (and films like *Inside Out*), the way to do this is through emotion, in order to activate the amygdala during the encoding of experiences. This tags the memory, so that it can be readily retrieved at any time in the future where a situation feels threatening, because it has been filed in the 'first aid' bit of the brain.

Vicarious learning

Another ancillary finding that we made was about vicarious learning. Given that there are many people who prefer to learn from the sidelines, because they find active participation in experiential learning too exposing, we worried that there was discrimination built into our choice of pedagogy. What we found, though, when we measured heart rate and learning was that the correlation between them held even when the participant had been watching a Critical Incident rather than participating in it directly. While heart rate tended to be higher for those in the hot seat each time – and, therefore, the degree of learning gleaned – as long as those watching felt involved enough for their own heart rate to be affected, they learned, too.

This is a really important finding, because both active and passive learners collude on training programmes about regarding 'reflective' learning as time off. Organizations certainly do – looking out of the window is not generally considered to be 'working'. And, in order to eke out valuable training spend, many Learning and Development departments think that the more contact time on courses, the better value for money. I do not want to conflate the activities of reflection and observation, but I do want to make a point about people who prefer to learn at one remove. Too often quiet learners are fobbed off with a brief walk or the opportunity to write some notes and that is that. They may even be forced into active learning exercises, on the grounds that it is good for them to feel their learning edge. Thus, our neurobiology findings are a triumph for people who hate the limelight so much they will avoid learning opportunities that require it – because this research shows you how you can opt in and opt out at the same time.

Here is an example. You and a colleague are both really struggling with someone in your team. You have had a lot of whinge sessions by the water cooler and over the odd drink after work and your colleague reckons it is time to tackle the thing head on. You could just say 'Good luck, mate, not my thing'. Or you could agree that you will coach them through it, attend the meeting as moral support and give them feedback afterwards about how you thought they did. Your heart would certainly be going like the clappers while you watched your colleague edge their way through. And if you ever did have to have a tricky conversation in your own right, you would have gained the neurobiological muscle memory you need to feel resourced to do so.

Alternatively, you might simply focus on raising either your level of investment in a work situation, or the risk that you might be called upon to get involved. So you could help plan an event or write a speech or offer to be a colleague's emergency expert if they get stuck in a tricky Q&A. You could even agree to understudy for a colleague who is worried about taking something on in case the dates do not ultimately work out. Anything, in fact, that makes you as an observer feel slightly on the edge of your seat. Because what our research showed was that if your heart rate is raised by your emotional investment in the situation, you will learn from it.

10,000 hours

It is probably also worth saying something about how our findings relate to Malcolm Gladwell's '10,000 hours' hypothesis. Introduced by Gladwell in his 2008 book *Outliers*, the '10,000 hours' rule holds that the key to achieving world-class expertise in any skill is largely a matter of 10,000 hours of practice. This idea, based on the work of Swedish psychologist K. Anders Ericsson, argues that there is no such thing as 'genius', just a lot of hard work and repetition. This is what produces the art that conceals art: hours of practice seem to be the only way to embed something so deeply that the art appears artless. Extrapolating this into the field of leadership, there has been a lot of argument historically about 'great men' and whether leaders are born or made. The '10,000 hours' rule suggests that anyone who puts in that degree of practice on the Critical Incidents we have identified would be a great leader. However, most of the future leaders I have met do not have this kind of time. Taking a neurobiological shortcut, courtesy of templating, cuts this down drastically. If 10,000 hours is like laying down synaptical connections that start as a sheep trail and with repetition become a path, then a lane, then a track, then a road, then a motorway, amygdala-based learning is like sending in the heavy machinery to cut straight to the motorway.

Learning to learn

In his groundbreaking book, *Probably Approximately Correct*, Harvard's Leslie Valiant argues that Darwin's theory of evolution crucially neglected the role of learning. We know the what – adaptation – but how? He answers this question with the notion of ecorithms – algorithms that learn from interaction with their environment. As a species, we have evolved by learning. And as a species, if we do not keep learning, we are not adapting, which threatens our future survival. So, to round off this chapter on learning, here is my primer on how to learn. If you are already on top of this, do skip straight on; or come back to it when you are about to start your next development experience. Here are my 3Rs of adult learning: Receptiveness, Retention and Retrieval. All three need to work for learning to be acquired, retained and usable.

Receptiveness

Receptiveness is about *salience* and *arousal*.

Salience? Over time, our brains get increasingly full and efficient and will not get out of bed for old hat. So the learning needs to appeal to our survival instinct. First, is this new? Novelty appeals to the collector instinct in your brain. Then, how will this knowledge help me this week, next week, when? If it does not appear useful, your brain is not incentivized to invest precious processing capacity on it. So if you are ever in a learning environment where you are struggling to see the point, make a fuss until you can or try another route.

Arousal. If your brain is busy processing food, fighting sleep, expelling toxins or firing off antibodies, it cannot help you. Paying attention to your physical capacity to learn stops you wasting time. This is an occupational hazard on residential training courses – mega-meal carb-loading makes you too sleepy to learn and late-night bar-bonding means you sleep so poorly that you do not convert the day's learning into memories. Yet another reason why learning on the job is often more effective. And, if you are ill, do not be a hero – wait until you are better. If you do feel sluggish, lab research and old wives' tales, as immortalized in unpopular boarding school rituals, suggest that a morning run or other vigorous cardio-vascular activity speeds your brain up. As we have seen, you literally get faster at reading and problem-solving after ten minutes of heart rate-raising exercise.

Retention

Is the learning structured for memory? Ashridge's memory expert Vicki Culpin has a useful mnemonic for retention – MARC – encapsulating the four key principles necessary to ensure effective storage in long-term memory: Meaning (the organization of material, building on previous knowledge), Attention (effort and motivation), Repetition (rehearsal) and Creativity (distinctiveness and uniqueness).

If you are optimizing your learning for retention, you need first to make it **Meaningful** for you. This requires some crunching and chewing, and the asking of awkward questions about relevance. You need to kick the tyres and not take everything on trust, because you need actively to make some shelf-room for this learning inside your head. As we have seen, if you can tag it as a new and particularly useful piece of learning, your brain will be naturally keen on it. If not, you will need to hang it next to a similar outfit, so your brain can find it easily in the future. This meaning-making is why teachers secretly love awkward customers. That ostensibly annoying vocal struggling with new insights is actually a sign of effective learning, so it is usually feedback that the process is working.

We have already talked about **Attention** in the context of arousal, but here it is also about focusing that attention more exactly. Apparently, healthy people do not usually get more forgetful with age, they just stop paying attention, because they have seen or heard it all before. And you cannot expect to be able to retrieve a memory you did not create in the first place. If you notice your mind wandering, tempt it back with novelty. If the person you are listening to is boring, ask a question, or try to write down everything you have picked up so far. Or start planning when you will next deploy this information or knowledge, or learn about how not to present by observing keenly their precise effect on the room. As soon as you can, take a break, drink some water and come back ready to re-engage. This is where self-directed learning wins out, because you can pace yourself better digesting short TED talks or small chunks of audio books more readily than you can fast forward a live presentation.

For the **Repetition** element, Culpin reports that short-term or 'working' memory only lasts for around fifteen seconds. To transfer it into longer-term memory requires rehearsal. Even the act of saying it out loud will help, because it uses more of your brain than just listening. This is why passing something straight on tends to be such a strong way to learn.

The final element of the MARC model is **Creativity**. The more you can play around with the memory, the stronger it will become, because more connections are made in the brain. My Very Excellent Mother Just Served Up Nine Pizzas was the way I learned the original order of the planets; you may have learned the rainbow as Richard Of York Gave Battle In Vain. Did you know that a litre of water's a pint and three-quarters; and a metre measures three foot three inches, it's longer than a yard, you see. These homely ways of learning sequences and dates and rules work because they are creative. They use memorable words and phrases, stories or rhyme. So MARC is a good way to structure for retention. Now, back to the 3Rs.

Retrieval

The final 'R' in my 3Rs for grow-ups is Retrieval: the whole point and proof of learning. When you need your learning, your brain will go searching for it. There is a lot of stuff in there already, so the more you can do to tag your memories, the easier it will be for your brain to find them again. As we have seen, the thinking on learning under pressure is that your brain codes these memories with emotion. You can do this without pressure by consulting books on memory techniques and by learning in as multi-sensory a way as possible, to increase the sheer volume of tags to facilitate rediscovery. But without pressure, the quickest way I have found to learn something is to teach it, as soon afterwards as you can. Even if you fudge this a little by writing a blog about it, or recording a quick video of yourself explaining it for your mates on Facebook. Because intending to teach it means you are likely to get really busy trying to understand it, by asking awkward questions and taking the sorts of notes that would help you to transfer the knowledge on. But for supreme confidence you cannot beat templating under pressure, because when you are under pressure these memories are naturally prioritized for you.

Now we know what leaders need to know and how they learn. Done? Not quite. I think there is another piece of the jigsaw and it is about the notion of character, because character is what future-proofs your ability to lead.

Chapter 3

Character

Most leaders I know would like to feel more confident. Indeed, the reason I have written this book is to give you a route map for that journey. I wonder whether confidence is the best goal, though. I think character is a better one. If, for any reason, you ever lose confidence, character is all you have left to fall back on. Character protects your future ability to lead because it is the very thing that will save you when everything else is stripped away. Courage, grit, determination – these character traits are the stuff of leadership when the chips are down. While confidence can be faked, character is real. This chapter sets out the case for character and explains why a templating approach can help you simultaneously improve your confidence and hone your character.

Remember the name Richard Farrington. He is a great case study and role model for leaders. In 2002, he was commanding the Royal Navy destroyer *HMS Nottingham* when it hit Wolf Rock, a clearly marked reef off Lord Howe Island in the Tasman Sea. Ashen-faced, he told the media:

> Just as the sun comes up in the morning, if you run your ship aground you get court-martialed. It hazarded the lives of 250 men and women. We have done significant damage to a major British warship. This is quite the worst thing that's ever happened, quite the worst character-building stuff. I'd say it's the worst feeling in the world.

As events turned out, he was following that time-honoured tradition – that many modern leaders seem to have forgotten – of taking responsibility. In fact, he had left the vessel to accompany one of his men to hospital, leaving a lieutenant in charge. It was the lieutenant's decision that had caused the ship to run aground, but the Commander had asked that the statement he had delivered on-site, in which he took full responsibility, should be the one adopted by the MOD, in order to protect his man.

What is character?

Did you ever complain about playing games in the rain, only to be told by your parents that it was 'good for the character?' What does that mean, anyway? Would not a person who usually follows the rules, or gets good results, be a person of good character? Not exactly. One person who has written extensively about character in the modern period is Alasdair MacIntyre. In his book, *After Virtue*, he tries to explain behaving virtuously as the difference between doing something for the extrinsic or instrumental rewards it could give you, or doing it just because it is a good thing to do in and of itself. Art for the sake of art. To illustrate this, he uses an analogy of painting. By painting a portrait, the artist is given an external reward (payment or fame), but in paying deep attention to its quality and excellence beyond that which might be required to generate this external reward, the artist also contributes to the general professional practice of portrait-painting, an internal reward or good in itself.

This is what the writer Dorothy L Sayers describes as 'serving the work', not serving the community. In the 1942 essay *Why Work?*, she worries that an addiction to 'service' makes us slaves to feedback, unable to discern the inherent quality of work for work's sake. If we constantly have one eye on our audience, we do not have both eyes on the work. And if we establish a psychological contract that expects approval or at least some appreciation for our pains, we set ourselves up for disappointment if the reward does not quite match up, which also devalues the work. Finally, we become victims of fashion, with no enduring idea of quality, because it becomes an entirely moveable feast. In some ways, this was the old distinction between the professions and industry – the professions prided themselves on absolute standards of excellence that were upheld and policed by them; industry was free to produce whatever good or service would find favour with the customer, and excellence was in the eye of the beholder.

Perhaps in the context of leading you could couch these as leading versus role modelling: in the case of the latter you are aware of a wider audience, both in time and space. You are in some senses dancing ahead of yourself and looking back to see how your act echoes in eternity.

Mere portrait painting MacIntyre describes as 'contingent'. You paint the portrait or take the lead because of what you might get back. He was a brave man ... when it looked like a good idea. He was a wise man ... when things went his way. He was a good man ... when it looked worth his while to be so. MacIntyre says that we cannot be genuinely courageous or truthful and be so only on occasion. Contingency introduces both a level of conditionality and a level of selfishness into the equation. When we meet virtuous people, people of 'good character', there is something durable and reliable about them. Their values are the core of their being. They cannot avoid being virtuous, it is somehow in their DNA. Character is not about doing but about being. It is not an activity, but an intrinsic property. That is why, when a kind person is catty, we say 'that was out of character'.

This brand, this guarantee of virtue and honour, is extraordinarily powerful. Yet it is so easily destroyed by one selfish act or bad decision. We punish our heroes if they let us down through deliberate actions or through circumstance. Equally, in the same way that a complaining customer who is dealt with well will tend to become increasingly loyal to the brand, tests of character not only strengthen the leader, but strengthen their brand by reinforcing it in adversity. We know the power of this because we have preserved it in our mythology. All wisdom traditions have tales of trials, where a hero has to be tested and found true. The Labours of Hercules, princes slaying dragons, hobbits ring-bearing – each trial represents what Sir Edmund Hillary described when he said: 'it is not the mountain we conquer, but ourselves'. They are what the character expert David Brooks would call those 'crucible moments', when we need to be tried in the fire in order to achieve purity.

Hallmarks

If you examine a high-quality piece of jewellery or an object wrought in silver, gold, platinum or palladium, it bears a hallmark. These symbols and letters are stamped into the metal to tell you who made it, where it is from and the quality of the metal used. The relevant Assay Office still carries out the hallmarking centrally to quality-assure the precious metals employed. Generations on and family heirlooms still bear their hallmarks, deeply etched. They attest perennially to the quality of the item. A hallmark is like the writing running through a stick of rock – it is what defines you as a leader. This is the stuff you are made of. In this context, it becomes the essence of your personal brand. When the signals from your surroundings are weak and your confidence fails you, all you have to fall back on is your essence, your character. It is all you have left when everything else falls away.

Character matters more than ever. This is because we are wholly overwhelmed with information, which forces us to be selective. This means we have to be good at choosing. And for all the reasons we have mentioned, leaders are vulnerable, because they are supposed to show strong leadership in the face of uncertainty and to provide followers with a sense of clarity and direction. If they do not, they have a tendency to get replaced. So leaders need to be grounded in a deep sense of values and purpose so that they do not lose their bearings. And they need to make wise choices.

Kurt Hahn, who founded the Scottish independent school Gordonstoun gave it a wonderful motto: *'plus est en vous'*, which trans-lates as 'there is more in you (than you think)'. Generations of pupils there have participated in a curriculum which is designed to inculcate character, through challenge, service and responsibility, both within the classroom and beyond. Whether they are stranded on a mountain in the snow, sailing in gale-force winds, blue-lighting in the school's fire engine or volunteering in the community, Gordonstoun pupils are encouraged to dig deep to discover the 'more' that is in them across a wide variety of demanding settings. Knowing what we now know about challenge learning, it is clear why this kind of an education works, and why this deliberate laying down of emotional experiences generates such resourceful alumni.

Nowadays, the promotion in schools of 'character education' is government policy, because the body of evidence in its favour is so strong. Thanks to the work of centres like Demos and the Jubilee Centre for Character and Virtues at the University of Birmingham, we know that character not only correlates with educational attainment, it correlates with well-being, mental and physical health, and success in employment. Crucially for government, it delivers better citizens, through the development of moral and civic virtue. Of course, the intellectual argument for attending to character has always existed, but modern policy tends to need an evidence base before it develops teeth. This shift in government policy is good news for future leaders, but it also serves as a reminder to existing leaders to look again at their own character formation and revisit it in the light of their role as a leader.

Virtue ethics

In academia, character shows up as an enthusiastic rediscovery of the Aristotelian idea of virtue ethics. Virtue ethics contrasts with systems of morality based on rules or consequences, on the basis that it is less about obeying laws or playing the odds and more about durable habits and character traits. It is about virtue for virtue's sake: virtue as its own reward.

To our modern ear, this may sound a bit silly. Would it not make more sense to do or not do something because of the consequences of it? Or because of your allegiance to some code of living? However, virtue ethics is hugely sophisticated, seen retrospectively through the eyes of modern neurobiology. As Aristotle himself puts it in his *Nicomachean Ethics*: 'we become just by doing what is just, temperate by doing what is temperate and brave by doing brave deeds'. We now know that this is neurobiologically true: if you change your behaviour, you will rewire your brain.

A man lies injured in the road. Passers-by who have a rule-based morality will help because they believe in a maxim such as 'do as you will be done by', and they would hope to be rescued in a similar plight. People who live by an ethic of optimizing outcomes will help because, by doing so, it will improve the lot of the victim and possibly their own, by showing their altruism. Aristotle would help, because to do so would be virtuous, and it would allow him to exercise the moral practice of benevolence or mercy.

Of course, character is built up over time as the cumulative effect of a series of decisions and behaviours, so it could in theory be informed by either a rule or consequence-based ethic. However, the emphasis in virtue ethics is not about the reactive optimizing of individual decision-making, it is about the deliberate and proactive development of moral character. So my hunch is that the deliberate or accidental accumulation of experiences and behavioural templating is actually what we mean when we say 'character'. Like pearls, our lustre and the beauty of our nature come from this defensive softening of irritants through layers of meaning-making over time.

Eulogy virtues

For leaders this is hard work, but less risky than the alternatives. A leader who subscribes to a rule-based morality would improve themselves by getting ever better at learning and interpreting rules. This breeds a degree of legalistic sophistication, but does not help leaders to see when rules should be revised, re-negotiated, or virtuously disobeyed. The diligent consequentialist would hone their morality by getting ever better at reading the future to improve their ability to calculate outcomes. This future-scanning is useful, but it extrapolates from the past so can be blindsided by novelty. It also provides no nourishment when good decisions turn bad. There is some nobility – if also naivety – in obeying a rule even if it leads to failure. However, a bad call makes a leader look foolish or weak, even if the decision made looked robust at the time. History is a harsh judge, and many a statesman walks the halls of history trying to atone for decisions made on their watch whose consequences they now find hard to stomach.

Working on your character as a leader enlarges these narratives by including them but also transcending them through proactivity. Virtuous leaders are not blind to rules or consequences, but do not restrict or confine ethics to them. They do not wait for an ethical dilemma to present itself for resolution, they bake in daily ethical practice so that such events become humdrum and reflexive, rather than case studies for a future MBA class.

David Brooks calls this the pursuit of 'eulogy virtues'. In his book, *The Road to Character*, he argues that we have been duped into pursuing 'resumé virtues' instead, but that these are empty if they are not supported by the depth of a good character. This may be why it is now so trendy to start MBA programmes by asking participants to write their own eulogy, because inevitably in the final analysis we yearn for plaudits to do with generosity or kindness or love, not just of career success and material wealth.

Future-proofing

My colleague Chris Nichols uses a metaphor in strategy about whether you are sailing to France or discovering the Northwest Passage. In the case of the former, it is on the map; it is a common journey and tides and hazards are largely known. You chart a course and you sail there. Yes, there may be squalls or pirates, but these you can plan for. And that magic line on your map shows you at any time how far off-course you have gone and how to correct for your destination. Morality can be similar. Laws and rules of thumb have been developed down the centuries and internationally across the wisdom and legal traditions to give you the best possible framework for known dilemmas and quandaries. The utilitarian tradition of calculating outcomes allows you then to correct if you are blown off course by reality, or at least to generate fresh rules for next time. But the Northwest Passage? There be dragons. It may not even exist. All you can do is get the best boat, the best crew and as many tools and resources as you can safely carry, for any eventuality that may arise. You will also take to lurking around taverns listening to tall tales from old sea dogs in case there is any wisdom in them, and collecting fragments of faded maps that might perhaps contain a vital clue at just the right time. The emphasis is on readiness and maximizing your potential to greet evenly whatever you might encounter on the way. A bit like this notion of 20:20 foresight and leadership muscle memory, come to think of it.

Developing a truly rounded character that is ready for anything is a hard discipline, because it requires a commitment to the development of a whole range of virtues. Many of them may or may not see frequent use, but they all need to be supple. There is a famously devastating example of the importance of this. In the 1960s, the psychologist Stanley Milgram wanted to understand why, in the context of the Holocaust, so many people had behaved so very badly. The Milgram experiments involved a set of volunteers teaching word pairs to actors in an adjacent room who they thought were fellow volunteers. If the 'pupil' got an answer wrong, the 'teacher' had to administer an electric shock, with the voltage increasing in 15-volt increments for each wrong answer. The actors were issued with tape-recorded reactions of screams and pleading and encouraged to bang on the wall and protest as the shocks increased, then to fall silent. In some versions of the experiment, the teacher was prewarned that the pupil suffered from a heart condition. While many of the teachers did respond to these protests and question the purpose of the experiment, most continued after being told firmly by the experimenter that they must go on and that they would not be held responsible for their actions. The experiment was halted only if the teacher continued to question the experimenter after being told to continue four times or when they had administered the maximum 450-volt shock three times in succession. In a poll conducted beforehand, Milgram established a general prediction that an average of just over 1 per cent of the 'teachers' would progress the experiments beyond a very strong shock. In fact, Milgram found that 65 per cent of the teachers administered the experiment's final massive 450-volt shock, even though many of them were clearly very uncomfortable about doing so and every single one of them questioned the experiment at some point.

One reading of the Milgram experiments is that they showcase our capacity for cruelty. But the American philosopher Robert Solomon argues instead that the experiments show, in practice, how hard it is to prioritize warring virtues, particularly if one is more 'supple' than the other. He sees it not as a lack of character in the 'teachers', but actually a conflict of character traits. In the Milgram experiments, the war was between obedience to authority and human compassion. In the average human life, there are many more opportunities to practise obedience to authority than there are to practise compassion, making this virtue comparatively flabby. And current thinking in neurobiology about the 'plasticity' of the brain would support the idea that a given virtue needs to be actively practised in order for it to stick. If a virtue is not practised, our neural map for the virtue lapses, so the development of moral character can now be seen as the acquisition of a skill just like any other.

Incidentally, this gives a vote for the humanities subjects through the back door. Recently, there was an alarming report about the typical educational background of terrorists. The British Council wanted to look at whether better levels of education would reduce a tendency for people to be attracted to terrorism and found, to the contrary, that terrorists tend to be highly qualified already, in largely STEM subjects: Science, Technology, Engineering and Mathematics. A 2007 study by Gambetta and Hertog had already found that almost half of all known jihadis were university graduates, 44 per cent of whom had studied engineering. In the group more widely, there is a general bias towards technical subjects, which is now being reinforced by the banning of subjects like law, political science and philosophy from the curricula by the Islamic State of Iraq and the Levant in the areas it controls. Experts think that a black-and-white mindset, reinforced by the way STEM subjects are taught and examined, is morally problematic. As we discover more about brain plasticity, this need for constant puzzling over shades of grey makes more sense, as a vital discipline to keep our ethical maps fresh. As the ethicist Nigel Biggar has argued, humanities subjects have a vital role to play in the moral formation of discernment and good choosing, because, unlike the more quantitative subjects, they require the development of sophisticated reasoning and the ability to make compelling arguments about qualitative matters.

Leaders, therefore, need to develop character in general, as well as muscle memory for more specific leadership tasks. This is because strengthening your character will future-proof your craft, for the time when something new and unexpected occurs, for which you have no template. It reduces the risk for you as a leader. The snag about developing character is that almost by definition it takes time. Is there any way to make character development efficient, too? Well, the good thing about focusing on your craft for your craft's sake is that this in itself is a character-building exercise. And both the development of muscle memory for specific activities and the honing of the virtues is about steady templating over time. So you can develop both in parallel. The best way I have found to describe what this discipline is like is to look at a craftsman or a smith and to consider their journey towards mastery.

Chapter 4

Leadersmithing

We have looked at what leaders need to learn, how they can do it most efficiently, and why character is so important. Before we move on to the practical application of this in the second half of the book, I want to take a historical detour to see what we can learn from the tradition of apprenticing and the notion of apprentice pieces in particular.

First, where did my term 'leadersmithing' come from? Well, I was playing with the idea of muscle memory and Critical Incidents, and pressure and simulation, when in 2009 my sister got married to a man named Smith. In her wedding speech, she quoted the writer G. K. Chesterton:

> In most cases the name is unpoetical, although the fact is poetical. In the case of Smith, the name is so poetical that it must be an arduous and heroic matter for the man to live up to it ... The brute repose of Nature, the passionate cunning of man, the strongest of earthly metals, the weirdest of earthly elements, the unconquerable iron subdued by its only conqueror, the wheel and the ploughshare, the sword and the steam-hammer, the arraying of armies and the whole legend of arms, all these things are written, briefly indeed, but quite legibly, on the visiting-card of Mr Smith.
>
> G. K. Chesterton, Heretics

Leadersmithing, I thought – that is what I do.

I grew up in St Andrews in Scotland and sang in the choir at a church called All Saints. It had been built by Lady Younger as a mission to the fisherfolk. Some of the masons who had worked on it were still around in my childhood. The Lady Chapel in particular is a rhapsody in marble. One day the rector gave me a present, a small marble font, made of the same stuff used in the church. Having used it for years as an ornament, I came to realize it was an apprentice piece, maybe employed as a sales pitch, either for the marble to be used in the church or for one of the young masons to be employed to work it. Many years later, I was teaching some Clore Leaders from the cultural sector. One of them happened to be Head of Earth Collections at the Oxford University Museum of Natural History. 'That's a Cadgwith Font!' she said, 'We have one in our collection, too.' The font is made of serpentine, a soft marble containing magnesium and asbestos, which in Britain is only found in Cornwall. It was a tradition of those working serpentine from the Lizard Peninsula to copy the font from the local church at Cadgwith in miniature.

It is the perfect metaphor. If you can do something beautifully in miniature, it convinces both you and your masters that you are ready for bigger things. It is also efficient. You do not waste materials and you use carefully thought-out 'pieces' to test your ability to take all the elements you have learned about materials and tools, turning and polishing, and integrate them into a whole. And until the great university takeover, we knew this. It was always the tradition in workplaces to learn your trade at the feet of a master. After apprentice-ships morphed and changed in the face of the Industrial Revolution and its aftermath, the technical colleges used converging technologies and economies of scale to replicate this type of learning in the form of one-to-many practical training courses. Then they all became univer-sities and the rest is history. Now you need a PhD to get a job making the tea and, in the process, we lost something important. But what does it mean to be an apprentice?

Apprenticeships

I first learned what an apprentice was from the 1940 Disney classic *Fantasia*, which is a retelling of Goethe's 1797 poem 'The Sorcerer's Apprentice'. The story starts when an old sorcerer goes out, leaving his apprentice – Mickey Mouse – in the workshop with boring chores. Tired of fetching buckets of water, the apprentice enchants a broom to do the work for him, but he uses magic that he does not yet under-stand, and the broom's diligence means that the floor soon floods. Not knowing how to stop the broom, the apprentice tries to chop it up with an axe, but each piece becomes a new broom and takes up its own bucket, fetching more and more water. Eventually, the sorcerer returns and breaks the spell.

As it turns out, this is a rather brilliant depiction of the life of an apprentice. The first part of the seven-year training seemed invariably to consist of meaningless drudgery and it was only towards the culmination of the training that most apprentices were allowed to learn anything at all. Let me, therefore, say that I am not pushing smithing as a cunning way to reconcile yourself to tedious work. However, the traditional process for learning what was traditionally called the 'art and mystery' of your trade does still have salience for those seeking to learn how to lead.

Apprenticeship used to be the main way you entered trade. In England it was made the compulsory route in the Statute of Artificers of 1562. Once you hit fourteen years old, your parents would pay to have you indentured and you would leave home to spend seven years living with your master as a member of his household. They would feed, clothe and train you, until you were able to set up for yourself in the trade. The premiums paid by your parents varied depending on the trade. In 1747, the most expensive was a soap-boiling apprenticeship that cost between £100 and £200. Learning to become a banker or mercer cost £50, and it cost £20 to learn how to become an attorney or jeweller. Rather cheaper than boarding school.

The scheme was a fairly advanced piece of social engineering, because you could not employ a child unless you apprenticed them. Anyone under 21 who was unemployed could be indentured as an apprentice by the authorities, together with orphans and the children of the poor. Some parishes used this as a clever way of outsourcing their own poor to other regions, where the indenture would require them to be fed, clothed and housed by their master rather than by the parish council, and at least by the time they emerged the poor would have the means to become economically productive. So the law on apprenticeships effectively protected children and was policed by the guilds, removing this burden from the state. It was cheap labour, too, and there was some sharp practice about letting apprentices go when they had served their term, in order to avoid having to pay them properly. However, the system survived largely intact for hundreds of years because it generally worked.

It is hard to estimate the scale of apprenticing, either as an absolute figure or as a percentage of the population. Historians Joan Lane and

James Ayres variously estimate that there were 11,000 and 30,000 apprentices, in London by the 1690s. As the population of London at the time was around 500,000, in either case they made up a significant proportion – and were significant enough a proportion to create problems. Usually this was youthful high spirits, in defiance of the indenture ban on their frequenting of public houses or brothels, which drew them like moths to a flame. Occasionally, this was rather darker, and manifested itself in several apprentice riots. As Lane recounts, one of them took place on Evil May Day in 1517, when 1,000 apprentices rioted against foreign traders in the City. They freed prisoners who had been locked up for attacking foreigners and marched on the parish of St Martin's Le Grand, where many foreigners lived. Houses were looted and the rioting went on until 3 a.m., with 300 arrests. Thirteen of the rioters were convicted of treason and were executed.

The working day of an apprentice was long, and they did not get much time off. For artificers, and labourers hired by the day or week, the working day was defined by the Statute of Artificers and it is unlikely that apprentices got a better deal. Writing in 1912, the historian Jocelyn Dunlop reports that, from March to September, the typical day started at 5 a.m. and finished around 8 p.m. In the winter, the working day stretched from the 'spring of the day until night', with 2.5 hours allowed for breakfast, dinner or drinking. Apprentices got Sundays, festivals and feast days off, but as they lived with their masters and were bound by indenture to avoid theatres, pubs, gaming and women, time off might not have been as much fun as one might suppose.

Much of what we know about apprentices comes from court records, which show what happened when the master–apprentice relationship broke down. Usually it was waywardness on the part of apprentices and neglect or abuse by their masters. For instance, the Goldsmiths' minutes of 4 August 1561 tell of the young apprentice Edward Shotbolt who was found stealing from his former master. The money was used 'upon apparel for a maid that he was in love withal:' a fine worsted frock, thick ruffed neckerchiefs and hand ruffs 'costly edged with gold lace and silver lace'. As punishment, these items were displayed around him as he sat in the stocks, to be shamed in the presence of the whole company of Goldsmiths.

The seven years must have felt like a long time. For the first few, you generally made tea, swept the floor and ran errands, in the same way you have seen the most junior modern hairdresser do while you are sitting captive in your chair. When you had shown your master that you were trustworthy, you were allowed to prepare tools and materials for the more skilled to work on. Eventually, you were trained up in the craft and finally exposed to customers and clients, but rather carefully so that you did not poach them on graduation. This process, of course, is rather similar to what you or I would have met with starting at work, when we were all hungry for the opportunity to show what we could do and dying to be let loose on some proper work.

We still do not really know what apprentices were actually taught. While manuscripts in private collections show that handwritten craft manuals and workshop pattern books certainly existed, James Ayres argues that these remained personal and informal until the 1720s. Some trades went more public with their trade secrets before this date, in response to the Great Fire of London in 1666, in order to assist with the rebuilding of the City. However, it is clear from reading minute books and correspondence that trade secrets were generally kept. Ayres quotes from a mid-eighteenth-century letter sent by a local builder to Earl Fitzwilliam which contained so much detail about the proposed work that the builder felt obliged to warn the earl that 'if it be made publick, I must expect to be condemn'd, both by Surveyors & Workmen ... for setting forth the Mystrey of every man's Business in so clear a light'.

Reading these words can make it all feel a world away, but many trades still run the apprenticeship model. Jamie Oliver and Gordon Ramsey started as apprentices in the catering trade; Stella McCartney and Alexander McQueen in fashion; Sir Ian McKellen in theatre and Laurence Graff in the diamond trade. The Goldsmiths Company is one of the only guilds that still runs on a similar model to that of its foundation. Modern goldsmiths, silversmiths and jewellers still train through apprenticeships and complete apprentice pieces to graduate. This has recently been formalized in the creation of a new building, the Goldsmiths' Centre in Clerkenwell, East London, to bring together trainee and working goldsmiths and those interested in jewellery, silversmithing and the related trades, in a community that works and learns together.

Apprentice pieces

The standard wording of the indenture stipulated that, as well as including you in his household, your master was to instruct you in the 'art and mystery' of their trade. It is very hard to discern any kind of curriculum, until manuals started becoming more popular in the early days of technical training colleges. This was largely to protect trade secrets and to protect apprenticeship, both as a system and as a source of cheap labour. Eventually the system of test work popular in Germany and France gained popularity in the UK, whereby an apprentice would present a 'proof piece' to the guild to demonstrate their skill and eligibility to join. This was also a good way for guilds to test the competence of foreigners before allowing them to trade locally. In France, this was a two-stage process. You presented your *chef d'oeuvre* at the end of your apprenticeship, then served as a journeyman for five to ten years, before presenting your *chef d'oeuvre élevé* to become a master. Around 1619, in the north of England, the woodworking trades required a 'humbling piece' to be laid before the masters for their inspection and judgement, and they were also called 'artpieces' or 'masterpieces'. It is interesting to note that in modern usage a 'masterpiece' tends to apply to a career highlight rather than to a student project. The modern equivalent is the practice of creating a student portfolio to show your range and skill.

So what did they make? The Needlemakers of London required 500 needles of various sizes. The Carlisle Shoemakers required four pairs of double-soled shoes. And the Framework Knitters' Company? A pair of silk stockings. Lane and Ayres have argued that the whole thing was a bit of a racket, designed to extract joining fees, free stock or extravagant ornaments. For instance, in 1668, Caius Cibber obtained admittance to the guild by carving a stone mermaid for the courtyard of the Leathersellers' Company and, in 1712, John Hunt of Northampton, apprenticed to Grinling Gibbons, got into his guild by carving a statue of King Charles II for All Saints Church.

A 'humbling' piece was a good term. It sounds as though the whole process was pretty humbling. One modern apprentice I know, a brave man starting a new trade in his retirement, told me a little about the discipline. In the first few months of his apprenticeship at a furniture workshop, he was only allowed near hand tools in order to learn about wood and about precision. He talks beautifully of the monotonous but strangely calming hours of planing, and the despair you feel if you plane the wood just that little bit too far and have to start all over again. He also talked about learning wood and how different woods behave, and how you learn to listen to the sounds they make as you work with them, so you can tell if you are about to plane too much off. I love the thought of applying this kind of thinking to our trade as leaders. What would it be like if we were this careful in learning how to work with people, learning to listen as carefully for the differences and the tiny cues they give if we push them that little bit too far? The patience that is needed to learn this way is extraordinary.

It is also a humbling piece because not every apprentice made it. Then, as now, some of that was to do with skill and a lot was to do with power and politics. Apprentices often had to half-graduate to journeyman status until the guild was ready to admit them as a master. Sometimes this was more to do with attempts to control supply and demand than it was to do with quality standards. Being a journeyman did give them some security, however, in that they could now be paid as craftsmen, and it was a standard part of progression in continental Europe. While the name derives from their being paid 'by the day', many also literally became journey men. Taking their indentures as proof of their training, they travelled to wherever work was available, or to where useful experience could be gained. They were expected to remain unmarried, and were effectively in limbo until they were admitted to a guild. Without this membership, they were not citizens. With it, they enjoyed 'freedom' in the community, which allowed them to trade and to own property, and afforded them protection.

While many traditional trades have been superceded and many guilds now spend down their historical wealth supporting charitable causes, some still retain something of their traditional role. In a nod to tradition, the Merchant Tailors have recently reintroduced something akin to an apprentice piece. Since 1998, tailoring students and apprentices compete annually for the guild's Golden Shears awards, by making a tailored outfit to be judged by the country's top bespoke tailors. The Merchant Tailors also publish an apprenticeship standard for bespoke tailoring. Other guilds have branched out. There not being such a thriving fur trade these days, the Skinners host some newer bedfellows, the Worshipful Company of Management Consultants and the Guild of HR Professionals.

As we have seen, the Goldsmiths is a rare guild that today carries out a very similar role to its historical one. They still assay gold for quality, take apprentices, and use apprentice pieces to test their skill. Their apprentice scheme has been running now for over 700 years. Historically, apprentices would be signed over to their master by a parent or guardian, and this Binding Ceremony still happens today. At the end of the apprenticeship, the apprentice presents their masterpiece at a Freedom Ceremony at Goldsmiths' Hall, in traditional language, attended by the Wardens of the Goldsmiths' Company, dressed in full traditional garb. Currently they have forty apprentices, on three- to five-year terms, apprenticed to Freemen of the Goldsmiths' Company and embedded in their master's workshop full-time. Each discipline (diamond mounting, silversmithing, hand engraving, polishing, setting, fine jewellery design and assaying) has its own range of skills which must be demonstrated through the masterpiece, and apprentices are expected to spend around 200 hours working on the piece. As Helen Dobson at the Goldsmiths' Centre explains:

> One of our apprentices who was recently made free was an Assay Office Technician and, through her time, completed additional training at the Goldsmiths' Centre as part of her Day Release. The skills she learnt through this allowed her not just to Hallmark an existing piece of work, but to produce an entire set of playing cards and holder in silver. She hand-engraved the picture cards, laser-engraved the number cards and presented them in their own Hallmarked box. The piece was exceptional and more than demonstrated the skills she had learnt during her apprenticeship.

Journeymen

I recall a Monet exhibition, in London, in 1999, that was hung chronologically. At the beginning, they showed some of his early works. These seemed mainly to be strange pastiches of realism or cubism, or some form of imitation until Monet found his own style. Then he raced around the world painting everything. It was not until much later in his career, in the 1880s, that he settled down to haystacks and Giverny, to show how he could paint the same scene so differently throughout the day and through the seasons. I think this journey has resonance for leadersmiths. Apprentices copy to experiment with style. Journeymen rush about mastering everything, and masters confine themselves to the skilful deployment of their trademark offering. I wonder which Monet stage characterizes you?

When I was at Deloitte, everyone wanted to make Partner. And if you only made it as far as Director, everyone knew you had been shunted off to a branch line and would go no further. In the literature, being a journeyman was considered to be a similarly limbo-like career cul-de-sac. Masters had the freedom of their city, so could set up shop. As an apprentice, you could not – you had to work for them instead. But to our modern eye this is not so very strange. Most of us are employed, not self-employed, and entrepreneurs are regarded as rogue and special. I have no idea whether a journeyman felt like a second-class citizen or not, but I do think they are a useful metaphor for contemporary leadersmiths. Being a master is pressure. You have the P&L. You eat or not, depending on receipts. A journeyman is employed, so they get paid regardless, and they have the freedom to experiment, as they are still learning. There is something terribly clean about just doing a day's work and getting paid for it without the complexities of vocation, meaning making and purpose.

The master

When Megan Reitz re-ran the original Future Leaders research five years on, all our findings held up and a new one emerged. It had appeared in our original research, but not strongly enough to attract our initial attention. When she probed further about learning, she uncovered the vital role of good boss/bad boss. It did not seem to matter which way round – they just needed to be extreme one way or the other. So sitting at the feet of a role model needs to be reinstated as the default for learning. Of late we have perhaps become too keen on the cost-effective skulking in front of a solitary screen or the making of learning pilgrimages away on a train to eat too much in a mullioned mansion. Of course, both of these can work if they are curated well, but too often they are a generic strategy rather than a focused intervention and are not robustly evaluated enough to inspire confidence.

I never really wanted to learn from all these old bosses. I thought I knew much better than them, but learn I did – because all young bucks are predestined to become reluctantly wise at the hands of their masters. The East has never forgotten this in the way that the West has, retaining terms like 'guru', 'sufu' or 'sensei' for their elders who have earned their status through mastery. In his 2009 book, *The Craftsman*, Richard Sennett says:

> In a workshop, the skills of the master can earn him or her the right to command and learning from and absorbing those skills can dignify the apprentice or journeyman's obedience ... The successful workshop will establish legitimate authority in the flesh, not in rights or duties set down on paper.

Of course, this is why I kicked against the traces so much, not being one blessed with the virtue of obedience. It did not feel like chess or the piano to me. With these pursuits, you know you need to learn the basics and the rules before you can play. And perhaps because there has been so much 'art and mystery' about what leaders actually do, it is easy for junior staff to think it looks easy and that anyone can do it from Day 1. Whether we welcome it, or do so consciously at the time, what we learn from what we see leaders do is exponentially more influential than anything they might ever say. Legitimate authority in the flesh. If I do not respect your skill, you will have to play the line management card to make me follow you and I will only do so with reference to my job description. Discretionary effort and organizational citizenship? Only available to these leaders who inspire you into wanting to follow them, by choice. Perhaps it is about submission to the craft, not to the master, given that these days we are not indentured in the same way.

Let us start with awful bosses. Can you really learn from them? Particularly so, because they evoke such negative (and therefore memorable) emotions in you. I know that the ones I have worked for made me vow never to follow their precedent. They also left me with such scars that I have a heightened response to any similar behaviour from colleagues today. I now run a mile from people who evoke the same reaction from me, even if the job on offer looks great. I would encourage you to do so, too. If your boss makes your life a misery, leave. No job is worth it. You are too precious and life is too short.

And, conversely, those great bosses? I found them so inspirational I would follow them anywhere. I seek out their like in my career to this day. Martin Elengorn, Ann O'Brien, Phil Hodgson and Mark Pegg. Two were like me, but two were not. All four were confident enough to let me get on with it and to provide me with air cover while I did so. They taught me that a good boss will make even a mundane job a joy. On the other hand, a terrible boss will ruin even the most inspiring job and make you feel doubly miserable.

We know from studies like the Gallup 12 that the role of the line manager makes or breaks performance. In impact studies on the transfer of learning, we know that learning stands or falls on the behaviour of the line manager on return. So perhaps we should acknowledge this more formally, by reinstituting the key role of the line manager as apprentice master. Luckily these days you do not need to take your apprentices home with you at night. But the discipline of apprenticeship is a great way to define the day-to-day role of the manager, as distinct from the role of HR and L&D and that of the individual learner themselves.

Quality?

There is something uncomfortable about masters and craft, because lurking behind this thinking is the idea that your master's assessment of your output is definitive. If it does not conform to their standards, it is deficient. And in the case of apprentice pieces, if it does not conform to the guild's standards, it is deficient. So where is the room for innovation and creativity? I got 42 per cent for an essay once. I was devastated. The question set was: 'Is Faith Opposed to Reason?' I had – in my view rather creatively – set about answering this through logic and reasoning, rather than building my case from the recommended reading which I had found rather turgid. But the feedback I got was that I had misunderstood the purpose of writing undergraduate essays. Like a good apprentice, I was supposed to read the sources and follow the form: weigh them up with great diligence, before in the last sentence or two chancing my own thoughts on the matter. The time to let it all hang out was at PhD stage, I was told. I, therefore, have a great deal of sympathy with Scott in the 1992 *Strictly Ballroom* movie, who gets punished for 'unauthorized' dance moves. Again, successive music teachers wrung their hands as I galloped off trying to play pieces without first mastering scales and studies, because they were boring and I was in a hurry to be a virtuoso. But running before you can walk is not mastery and the tried and tested discipline of apprenticeship lasted for hundreds of years because it proved its worth. It worked because of the rigour of practice and because it required at least the 10,000 hours of practice that Gladwell reckons is the benchmark for mastery.

While my leadersmithing approach is not nearly this slow, it does suggest some set pieces. Importantly, though, it does not tell you what a good Critical Incident looks like. Neurobiologically that does not matter. In fact, if you make a mess of any of the Critical Incidents we know the learning will be stronger. Relative ease is the crucial factor. What your brain finds challenging will depend on your own stress thresholds and even the smallest steps will provide you with muscle memory if they feel like giant strides to you. However, over time you will need to develop your own internal quality standards. Your parents probably told you that if a thing's worth doing, it's worth doing well. One occupational hazard of leadership is that as you get more senior it will become harder to gauge how well you are actually doing. So developing your own sense of what good looks like will become one of the only ways you can keep sane.

The thing that is so striking about apprentice pieces like my little font is their quality. If you look at the tiny joins, the fine work, every detail is perfect. It is a particular test of skill to do small things that well. I remember spending probably far too long blowing up PowerPoint slides to check that the lines really did meet up on all the graphics we produced. This felt like rather a labour of love until I saw our PowerPoints projected on to a large screen and realized you could see the detail of every join.

A bit like the word 'luxury', if a product is branded 'quality', we tend to assume quite the opposite. And quality has been turned into so many operational processes it is hard to remember what it really means. For me it is a character trait rather than an activity. If you achieve extraordinary quality in one aspect of your life but let things slip elsewhere, it is not a durable characteristic. And for your followers to trust you, you need to be consistently reliable. Additionally, a widely shared commitment to delivering quality work is one of the perennial marks of an engaged workforce.

External standards vary and are dependent on scrutiny. Developing a strong internal standard is more likely to keep you honest when no one is looking. The way you hone this muscle is about going the extra mile. This might be about drafting an important email and leaving it overnight so you can check it again before you send it. It might be about proofreading that report an extra time, so you can make sure there are no errors. It might be about scheduling time before meetings so you can read the papers properly, and time afterwards so that you can turn your notes into diaried actions.

One of my favourite books as a child was *Miss Know It All* by Carol Beach York. In the story, an amazingly clever lady comes to visit an orphanage to demonstrate her extraordinary powers to the girls. But she is wrong-footed by one of them asking her 'what is the largest room in the world?' She has to stay for weeks researching this question, to no avail. Then one of the girls asks Mr Not So Much, the director who visits the orphanage from time to time to tell them all off. 'Room for improvement' he barks. As a leader, a reputation for restless questing after quality is well worth having.

Part two

Practice

Chapter 5

Crafty Essentials

The first part of the book has laid out the foundations for an apprentice approach to developing leaders. We have looked at the research behind it, the kinds of Critical Incidents that typically test leaders, and why character is so important. We have also explored the metaphor of apprentice pieces, as a way of identifying acts of leadership that can be used both to test, prove and develop your skill as a leader. This second half of the book moves from the theory to the practice.

This part of this book looks at some of the basics that leaders need to be able to do with elegance and ease. These core practices are the equivalent of learning about tools and materials as an apprentice, before you combine them with your art and mystery to make craft items for public consumption. We could use a range of metaphors – toolboxes, doctors' bags, kitchen cupboards, the alphabet – we need to be familiar with all of our resources and have the skill to select the right tool for the job in hand.

The metaphor I favour is a deck of cards, so I will use that as my organizing scheme. This is partly because a deck contains fifty-two cards – one for each week of the year – so you can use this scheme to curate your on-going development. Equally, you can 'pick a card' to provide any given week with a focus, by way of refreshing your skill sets and keeping your learning muscles supple. The exercises vary both in length and intensity so that you can mix and match. I used to play cards a lot when I was young. Some games needed the whole pack. Some needed two packs. Some just needed a few cards. But it is always useful to have the full pack at your fingertips, for the days when the only card that could win the trick is the 2 of spades.

The full set of apprentice piece exercises are grouped into four suits, with each card split into two parts: a brief overview of 'The Idea' and a way to practise it through 'The Exercise'. The full set are tabulated at Appendix 3 and are replicated here as Table 2 for ease of reference. They are also mapped to the Critical Incidents in Appendix 1, so you can see which exercises would most help prepare you for each of the seventeen. These are your winning hands.

You may have heard the old saying: 'you cannot do much about the hand you are dealt, but you can choose how to play your cards'. Sometimes this is used to explain the difference between fate and free will. Sometimes it is used as a motivational slogan. Sometimes it is just a reminder that despite our readiness and preparation, life will always throw up new challenges.

For me, there will be some cards that tend to win you points in any game. There will be some cards that do not appear that useful, but are sometimes exactly the card you need to avoid losing. And you will have existing strategies, habits, skills and biases about many of them already. For anyone who wants a thorough workout, though, these are the disciplines that I would commend to help you lead with grace and skill. I have grouped the exercises by suit for convenience:

- My **Diamonds** are about sharpness. These exercises are about how you can hone yourself as a fully deployable resource in the full range of leadership situations.
- My **Clubs** look at your physical impact. Some look at your intrinsic health and some look at your impact on those around you.
- My **Spades** are largely practical tools and techniques for getting things done through others.
- My **Hearts** are all about putting others at their ease and being comfortable in social situations.

Being a delight to work with will tend to be your best bet for attracting excellent performance from others. As you read through, you might like to use the table in Appendix 3 to assess your level of confidence about each of the areas listed and to plan when you might next practise them. Each section also contains a suit table for your use. You may want to work through the table first, to focus your attention on where you feel least well resourced. Or you might start by focusing on fine-tuning your strengths. Or you may want to read all the way through before you decide where best to focus your efforts.

Table 2 The cards

Diamonds		Spades	
A♦	Your Strengths	A♠	Difficult Conversations
K♦	Effort	K♠	Numbers
Q♦	Uncertainty	Q♠	Creativity
J♦	Letting Go	J♠	Conflict
10♦	Improvisation	10♠	Remaining Competitive
9♦	Attention	9♠	Delegation
8♦	Mood	8♠	Communication
7♦	Composure	7♠	Public Speaking
6♦	Hope	6♠	Meetings
5♦	Initiative	5♠	Networking
4♦	Habits	4♠	Working the Room
3♦	Missing Person	3♠	Mystery Shopping
2♦	Role Models	2♠	MECE
Clubs		**Hearts**	
A♣	Work–Life Balance	A♥	Manners
K♣	Sleep	K♥	Trust
Q♣	Fuel	Q♥	Listening
J♣	Personal Brand	J♥	Questions
10♣	Change	10♥	Eye Contact
9♣	Reading Cultures	9♥	Storytelling
8♣	Power	8♥	Relationships
7♣	Control	7♥	Choreographed Conversations
6♣	Gravitas	6♥	Coaching
5♣	Posture	5♥	Teams
4♣	Sumptuary Law	4♥	Feedback
3♣	Colours	3♥	Thank yous
2♣	Social Media	2♥	Character

Chapter 6

Diamonds

Sharpening the saw

The first set of practices are my diamonds, because they are about sharpness. You may have heard that story about the man who meets a woodcutter, busy sawing logs in the forest. The woodcutter is exhausted and frustrated because his saw is blunt. The man suggests to the woodcutter that he stops and sharpens it. The woodcutter tells the man that he does not have time to stop. In his acclaimed book, *The 7 Habits of Highly Effective People*, Stephen Covey uses this idea of 'sharpening the saw' as his seventh habit. For leaders, you are the saw and your sharpness is dependent on how familiar you are with yourself as a resource and how well you are able to deploy yourself in the full range of leadership situations. You are no good to anyone if

Table 3 Diamonds

Diamonds		RAG	Next chance to practise
A♦	Your Strengths		
K♦	Effort		
Q♦	Uncertainty		
J♦	Letting Go		
10♦	Improvisation		
9♦	Attention		
8♦	Mood		
7♦	Composure		
6♦	Hope		
5♦	Initiative		
4♦	Habits		
3♦	Missing Person		
2♦	Role Models		

you are just a one-trick pony in this game. You will notice that many of these items shade into the cognate areas of Emotional Intelligence, mindfulness and well-being – all disciplines about learning how to optimize the extraordinary mix of history, experience, personality, character and purpose that has brought you to where you are today. Use Table 3 to self-score Red Amber Green (RAG) by suit as you read through each section.

Ace of Diamonds – your strengths

The idea

If you reflect back on the highlights of your career so far, I would wager they arise more from your skilful deployment of strengths, than your subduing of weaknesses. If you spend too much time correcting your weaknesses, you will average yourself out. Instead, muster your strengths. Hone them well, because they are the cornerstone of your brand. They are your ace in the hole.

The exercise

Start by listing your strengths. You may find these in 360 or other psychometric reports, in appraisal or performance reports, in interview feedback or references, in your own CV or in letters you have written to apply for jobs or promotion. Rank them if you can, in order of competence. What are the reasons for this ranking?

- Which ones most readily become overdone strengths, like confidence being perceived as arrogance?
- Are there common triggers that make you push too hard?
- Do you tend to be commonly misunderstood by certain types of people or in particular situations?
- Can you experiment with your 'volume button' next time you find yourself in one of these situations?

Try dialling it down one notch at a time and noticing any reaction you get, whether spoken or in the body language of the people around you. And what are you not so good at? What are your strategies for getting help in these areas? When you cannot delegate tasks that are not your strong point, where do you find the energy to give you the strength to work at them, and how could you improve your resourcefulness in this area?

If you are too modest to have found any strengths, try this instead. Identify three work relationships – past or present – that have brought out the best in you. Email each person, asking them if they could reply with a summary of three of your strengths, together with a brief story of a time when they saw you deploying each strength to best advantage. Keep these emails and re-read them regularly. Your boss may also be interested in them, at appraisal time. If you want to make the process more formal, you could ask these colleagues to leave this feedback as a recommendation on your LinkedIn profile.

King of Diamonds – effort

The idea

There is no point being absolutely fabulous if you are not able to be reliably so. It makes people trust you less if they are not quite sure whether you will be on form or not on any given day. A lighthouse that is temperamental risks lives. So having the mastery to run yourself well and consistently is pivotal to your success.

It is thanks to the brilliant Daniel Goleman that the term 'Emotional Intelligence' has entered the lexicon. The *Harvard Business Review* called it 'a revolutionary, paradigm-shattering idea' and the American Psychological Association gave Goleman a Lifetime Career Award for it. Much of this book could be recast in his terms, because he has made the case for the pivotal importance of good Emotional Intelligence for effective leading. I love the simplicity of the labels on his famous grid, but here I want to talk about the lines between them instead. This is because I think they are not just innocent lines. Often they are more like huge brick walls, that can only be scaled through massive effort.

This is his model of Emotional Intelligence, expressed in the grid format used by the Hay Group:

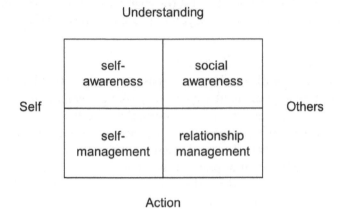

Figure 3 The emotional intelligence grid

Nowadays, Hay has turned this model into a psychometric tool and you can be tested to within an inch of your life about it, but I have a different challenge for you. It is about paying attention to the effort you need to make to be able to transition between the boxes with ease. Are you good at scrambling back and forth over the walls between them? Mastery here is the key to consistent performance. For example, I might be extremely aware that I am angry about something. What does it take for me not to give into that anger, to calm down and move on? Or say that I know my colleagues are feeling disconsolate. What does it take for me not just to join them in a therapeutic whinge, but to cheerlead them into cheerfulness instead? Can you grade these grid-lines red–amber–green so you are clearer where your primary development challenges lie? These will vary by situation and depending on the people involved, but are there some that for you are hot buttons? Can you pick one or two of them and decide to work on reducing the negative power they have over your performance?

The exercise

Here is a quick trick from the masters, for those days when you really do not feel like making an effort. The neuroscientists Kevin Ochsner at Columbia University and James Gross at Stanford University have shown that teaching people to reframe stimuli changes how they experience and react to them. You can train emotional regulation first by controlling attention to emotionally evocative stimuli, then by cognitively changing their meaning. In the jargon, this is to force a handback from the cortical and subcortical emotion-generative systems to the prefrontal and cingulate control systems. What?! Maria Konnikova explains it this way:

1 Change the situation to force perspective – if you cannot hang up, stand up; if you cannot walk away, suggest a walk with the person who has upset you. Call for a comfort break just to give you time to regroup. Distance yourself physically and in time if possible ('go home and sleep on it'), but otherwise use mental distancing. Hover above yourself and watch the action through a camera lens. Imagine how an onlooker would describe the scene. Ask yourself what you will think about this in hindsight.

2 Reappraise, reinterpret or reframe what has happened – force yourself to look for an upside, because this will in effect remove captaincy from your amygdala and return it to your rational brain. Which will in turn start calming you down and give you access to a wider range of options in how best to respond.

You can practise these skills by applying them around you whenever you notice that powerful emotions are kidnapping your staff. Rescue them by creating distance, then by reframing the situation for them: if Pollyanna was coaching you, what silver lining would she see in this situation? There are also a couple of tricks that work well on toddlers that you could try. Nowadays they think that tantrums are caused by asymmetric brain development during the terrible twos. This leads to a flooding of the brain by emotion that renders your typical toddler a heel-drumming mess on the pavement at the slightest provocation. One wise parent I know used immediately to ask his son 'what colour are foxes?' Similarly, when mine are grumpy, I tell them 'there's to be no smiling!' In both cases, the brain is tricked into a different response. Finding the colour red toggles the rational part of the brain back in, and trying deliberately not to smile ends up being funny. So you could always try asking overwrought colleagues boring stuff like times tables in case it throws them a life raft. But do not try a joke unless you are confident!

Queen of Diamonds – uncertainty

The idea

One of the Critical Incidents we identified in our research was about managing ambiguity and handling your response to uncertainty, but how can you improve your mastery in this area? The clearest framing of this I have seen is drawn from the work of Ralph Stacey, Professor of Management at Hertfordshire Business School, in the UK. Famous for pioneering the field of complexity, he is fond of contrasting two axes: agreement and certainty. Where things are close to both agreement and certainty, there is little ambiguity, but as things move away from either certainty or agreement, the more ambiguous they become. I think this neatly encapsulates the challenge. A leader's job is to nail down certainties and achieve agreement about them, wherever possible, so that the main effort can be directed to where it can add most value.

Here is a practical example. When I first worked with Counsel on a public inquiry, this was the model he adopted. Given the huge range of issues on which the parties were disagreeing, he identified all the ones that attracted certainty (costs, etc.) and where fruitful agreement might be reached. These were settled out of session, so that the Inquiry's time could be spent wrestling with those issues where certainty and agreement were hard to come by. This is your job: to spin off distracting but agreed and certain items, so you can spend time on the hard stuff.

If you want chapter and verse on this, in the leadership literature it has appeared in the United States as Ronald Heifetz's 'adaptive leadership', and in the UK as Keith Grint's 'wicked problems'. These are different ways of saying similar things about your ability to diagnose correctly: are you facing a puzzle or a problem? If it is a puzzle, like a crossword or Sudoku, there is a solution. If it is a problem, there may not be. Do not waste your time over-complicating a puzzle – get it solved. And do not imagine problems just need more legwork – they may not be susceptible to solution. You may have heard a version of this in Reinhold Niebuhr's Serenity Prayer: 'God, grant me the serenity to accept the things I cannot change, the courage to change the things I can, and the wisdom to know the difference.'

The exercise

Next time you face a challenge, ask just these two questions: what is certain? And what is already agreed? If you keep working these two angles, you will tease out the known from the unknown and can save your energy for the things that really matter: the search for new certainties and your diplomacy for new agreements. One caveat. People love certainty, so they will put pressure on you to provide it. Beware – it may be kindly meant, but if your wild stab at a solution proves wrong, they will not forgive you for it.

Jack of Diamonds – letting go

The idea

A complementary practice that will help you surf uncertainty is your ability to let go. If you are in any way typical of the general management population, this will be hard. Because it is likely that you have achieved the career success you have by taking control and solving problems. You will have been so consistently rewarded for these habits that they will have become instincts. And you are likely to feel impotent and weak if you fail to respond in this way to any new challenges that appear. Given how many leaders feel like imposters anyway, I generally see a spike in control behaviours from new leaders, as they struggle to credentialize. Most often, they immediately search out familiar things or things they can master to make themselves feel powerful, whether or not these are the right or most useful things to do. So you will have to carefully wean yourself off all this competence, so that you do not just have a massive wobble in confidence.

The exercise

Start small. Take home the next airplane eye-shield you collect. When everyone is out of the house, put it on and try navigating your way around familiar rooms. You could even try brushing your teeth or getting dressed blindfold. If you are feeling brave, have someone lead you while you are blindfolded – perhaps as part of a teambuild. Or just rather gently let someone else choose dinner/the holiday/what movie to see, just so you can feel these letting go muscles flutter a bit. At work you could stop checking everything and let others sign things off. You could delegate more by sending substitutes to meetings, or by rotating the chairing of them. Or you could deliberately become 'junior' in another sphere to practice the virtue of humility. Perhaps this could be through volunteering or learning a new skill. Learning how to ski as an adult was my most sobering lesson in letting go. Being a new parent is also a quick way to convince anyone of their total lack of competence, so offer to help with a newborn for the day if you need reminding.

10 of Diamonds – improvisation

The Idea

I once had a whole troupe of actors come to Ashridge to teach me how to deliver a Shakespearean sonnet. I think it was to help me with public speaking. But it just made me feel like that episode of *Blackadder* in which the Prince Regent suffers something similar. There are, of course, some leaders who need to be skilled in reading from an autocue, but most of us do not have speechwriters. Most of us do not know what we are going to say until we stand up to speak or have not had the luxury of preparation time when the finger points and we suddenly have to go in to bat. It was not until I worked with Neil Mullarkey from the Comedy Store that I found what I was looking for – improvisation. The disciplines of improv from acting and comedy are among the most useful training for leaders. What you learn through improv is that you are infinitely resourceful. You can be presented with any crazy scenario and if you follow some basic rules your brain will come through for you, serving up something plausible – and funny – at the same time. While it may not be a leader's job to make everyone laugh, the sense of managing an audience is the same. It is also the closest thing I have found to a 'fluid intelligence' workout.

In 1971, before neurobiology got trendy, Raymond Cattell drew a distinction between two types of human intelligence: crystallized and fluid. Crystallized intelligence is the lattice of learned information you hold in your head, your hard-drive of knowledge. Fluid intelligence is your capacity to mine this data – a bit like googling – and to abstract from it insight for new situations. Over time, good fluid intelligence acts as a ratchet on your crystallized intelligence, as new solutions get filed away for future use. This works a bit like the military's notion of Standard Operating Procedures. These get trained into you until they become instinctive and you can do things like strip down a machine-gun in forty seconds while talking to your colleague about Euclid's Third Postulate. And much of our early education feels a bit like this – the reciting of times tables and declensions. However, teaching leaders ever more facts to add to their existing data set is not smart nor efficient, whereas teaching leaders how to improve their ability to self-google future-proofs them. Improv flexes these muscles. Creativity and other thinking tools may also help, but improv is a good basic resourcefulness practice.

The exercise

You can practise this as a formal improv exercise with a willing partner, or you can just apply these rules to your very next work conversation. In her book, *Bossyboots*, Tina Fey sets out a useful summary of the rules:

1 Agree – always say 'yes'. The Rule of Agreement reminds you to respect what your partner has created and start from an open-minded place.
2 Say 'Yes and' ... agree; then, add something of your own. It is your responsibility to contribute and your offers are worthwhile.
3 Make statements – do not just ask questions, because this puts pressure on your partner to come up with all the answers. Be part of the solution instead, by offering suggestions.
4 There are no mistakes in improv – only opportunities and happy accidents. Your ability to respond well to the unexpected and unpromising is the difference between saving the scene or killing it.

Having used improv with many leaders over the years, there is great wisdom in these rules. The first two are a particular challenge for managers, invariably used to being rewarded for their critical faculties and for being good at spotting problems. 'Yes buttery' is a management classic and is probably why so many staff surveys complain that the higher-ups do not listen and why staff do not feel valued. Years of every suggestion being greeted by 'yes but' tends to shut people up. The bridging and building effect of 'yes and' immediately generates energy and possibility, even if you need to be fleet of foot about not getting a colleague's hopes up if they are living in a dream-world: 'yes, and you could draft a paper on that for the Board ...'.

The 'statements' rule is interesting for those who want to create impact. Tina Fey particularly recommends it to women who give away their authority by using questions as a way of softening statements, to avoid coming across as too pushy. In coaching, good questions will always have a place, but in normal conversation the offering of suggestions as well as the asking of questions shares the burden and helps promote partnership.

The final rule about there being 'no such thing as a mistake' is also salutary. Business life is littered with examples of 'mistakes' that became triumphs, from silly putty and post-it notes to penicillin and Viagra. Just recently a doctoral student discovered how to make a battery last forever, by accident. So maybe the next crazy thing a colleague says will become your new best product idea, if you respond well to it.

And, if you worry that by 'winging it' you will forget your lines or draw a blank, take some advice from a cabinetmaker and listen to the wood. If you trust the other person's eyes, they will tell you what to say next. Which conversation can you next try this in?

9 of Diamonds – attention

The idea

There is an extraordinary philosopher, Simone Weil, who starved herself to death in 1943 in solidarity with the Free French. She wrote extensively, but perhaps most beautifully on the topic of attention. Given how ubiquitous mindfulness is these days, her writings sound particularly apposite, because mindfulness is essentially about attention. We know from cognitive psychology that attention is about cognitive load. And we know that our generation is particularly vulnerable to it, because of the increase in information all around us. As Martin Hilbert's doctoral study showed, in 2011 we took in five times as much information every day as we did in 1986 – the equivalent of 175 newspapers per person per day. Frequent distractions and interruptions also increase cognitive load, which reduces our ability to do tasks well. This can also make us more likely to indulge in stereotyping and other bad habits of thought, because we start deploying heuristics and shortcuts to try to reduce load. Overload also has physical effects. Balance is adversely affected by high cognitive load and greater pupil dilation in the eyes is also found to be associated with it. So a lack of attention can make you bleary-eyed, wobbly, biased and error prone.

Weil has this to say about attention: 'the amount of creative genius in any period is strictly in proportion to the amount of extreme attention ... the capacity to drive a thought away once and for all is the gateway to eternity. The infinite in an instant.' In other words, if we clear our minds, we make room for new insight. In an essay written on education, she contends that the fostering of good attending skills should be the primary aim of all schooling, because whether or not our attention wins us victory in a maths problem, the skill of learning to attend will reap benefit right across the curriculum, as well as in life. This philosophical point, now well tested in cognitive psychology, is a timely reminder for leaders. Constant interruption and the vying for your time comes with the territory and if you are unable to focus your attention well, you will soon spread yourself so thinly you will be no good to anyone.

The exercise

The mindfulness experts will have you practise your focusing skills by gazing at an object in some detail, or using meditation tools to quieten your mind with your eyes closed. Colleagues like Megan Reitz at Ashridge are experts in this field. For leaders on the job, I would recommend this rough-and-ready routine next time you face an interruption and need to focus your attention: Eye contact. Listening. Love.

There is a scene in the 1999 movie *The Matrix* when the bullets heading towards Neo slow down. The visual effect they use in the movie is called Bullet Time. It allows the audience to 'walk round' an event happening in slow motion, to see it from different angles. I think this is what leaders need to be able to do. For me, eye contact is the first step. Your mind will follow, so what do you need to look at to attend well – a person, a screen, a scene? Give it your physical attention and mentally walk around it to keep focused.

Next, give it the attention of your mind. Listen with every ounce of your body – attend to tone, pitch, vocal quality, body language, pauses, throat-clearing, the choice of words, and what is unsaid. Notice your mind wandering and recall it by shifting your focus back through eye contact, or by varying which element in their delivery you attend to next. My Queen of Hearts exercise on levels of listening will help you with this.

Finally, love. Not a trendy word in leadership circles, but an underused one. Love is the reminder to let your ego slip free, so you can genuinely be of service in this moment. Let go of your need to respond well or to move things on. Rest in the eye of the storm. Behold the person or the situation and let time dissolve away. Einstein's time is relative, so allow it to stretch around you a little more. Hold the person or the situation like a butterfly in your hand. Let it settle before you open your mouth and disturb it again.

One of my colleagues talks about looking at data with 'soft eyes' and this is the effect you want. The military have a discipline of 'averted vision' – looking away so that your peripheral vision kicks in. Give your attention in this complete way, so that you can see the wood and the trees and be seen to be doing so. And smile, to remind both you and the person you are with that you are choosing to be there.

8 of Diamonds – mood

The idea
Mood is about the weather: the climate you create around you at work. Leaders cannot avoid affecting the culture in this way, so you might as well get it right. Too often leaders imagine their mood is a secret or that they are far too grown-up to suffer from moods. This just makes everyone collude in pretending you are moodless, which makes everything worse. You can diffuse all of this by naming your moods – even better by being so familiar with them you can orchestrate them rather than being conducted by them.

The exercise
How do you feel, reading this right now? Do you feel better or worse than you did half an hour ago? Draw a horizontal line across a page.

Imagine that is 'neutral'. Now think about your first moment waking up this morning. Were you above or below this line? Starting at the left, try to draw your mood so far today, above and below the line, as you got up, negotiated your way out of the house, travelled to work, got started and so on. Can you recall what made the line move up or down? Make notes both about your positive and negative triggers. Now think about anyone you came into contact with during this 'line' – do you remember them saying or doing anything that showed how they were reacting to you and your changes in mood? How could you tell what they were feeling? Now imagine you have the ability to reshoot this scene. What corrections would you make? Why?

7 of Diamonds – composure

The idea

I wonder how you feel watching your team or favourite player at a crunch point in the game. How can they look so composed when even you as a spectator are sitting there feeling a bit sick? You may recall the England rugby fly-half Jonny Wilkinson taking penalties. Arms outstretched, taking aim, eyes exactly in line; imagining the trajectory of the ball between the posts, staying calm, getting his pulse rate steady; then delivering incredible accuracy. A portrait of poise under pressure.

We feel uncomfortable watching, because emotional spikes are accompanied by a stress response in the body. That is why your Mum always told you to take a deep breath and count to ten. The idea behind this annoying advice is about stimulating the para-sympathetic nervous system, so that your body calms down and you feel better able to cope with the challenge you face. You can see top performers in any field visibly steeling themselves to remain composed under pressure.

Composure for leaders is essentially about appearing to stay in control of yourself. It worries people if you lose control and it undermines their faith in you. Anything from shouting in a meeting to gobbling up all the extra doughnuts, it suggests that you are not quite on top of things. Of course, this is about perception not reality – maybe if we were just screaming inside, people would not judge so harshly.

Are there patterns about when you tend to lose control? Think about the reputation you want to have and the example you most want to set for those around you. Is there anything visible that you do that undermines this or sends out mixed messages? Maybe there is an office nemesis who winds everyone up. Instead of ranting next time you hang up, could you draw or write down your feelings instead, to make them less public? Remember, this is not about suppressing your wholly legitimate feelings, it is about deploying them well and powerfully, so as best to improve the existing situation. So, cultivate your poker face and you will give yourself more choice about when you want to display emotion and when it would be more useful for you to keep it in check.

The exercise

Next time you feel your hackles rise:

Stop.

Breathe out.

If you feel too cross to start counting, start by breathing out, even if this manifests itself as a bit of a snort or a huff. Breathe out all the way and do not breathe in again until your body does it for you. Now, very deliberately, make yourself smile and relax into the smile until it feels natural. Now respond to the situation. Perhaps with a question? If it is a solicitous question, like 'did that come out a bit wrong?' or 'sorry, did that upset you?', that will really help, as altruism also stimulates the para-sympathetic nervous system. If you keep practising this 'Breathe out. Smile' routine it will become an automatic reaction, which will buy you valuable time to recalibrate when you are upset. Over time, you may be able to slow down the rate at which you react and become more inscrutable, which may help in situations where you need to manage your demeanour more exactly because of the effect your mood may have on others.

One quick trick that might help you with this is to be aware of this bizarre research. In 1988, Fritz Strack and colleagues found that people looking at cartoons found them funnier if their faces had been forced into a smile by having a pen in their mouth. So if you are really struggling, either bite down laterally on a finger, or pop your pen in your mouth – it will stop you saying anything rash and it will improve your mood.

6 of Diamonds – hope

The idea

Vision is often bracketed with strategy, as a summary or strapline for it. For the leader, it is important to remember that this is not some dusty planning activity. It is about offering hope. That is why they will follow you. So this is about how you remain hopeful and optimistic, as well as how you offer that hope to others.

When I was taught Latin and Greek, I had to learn about moods, which was a great way to learn more about our own language. What is this? Interrogative. What might this be? Subjunctive. Bored now. Indicative. Get on with it! Imperative. There were some I had not heard of though, like the locative, which is about place, and the optative, about wishing. These have now lapsed in the English language, but I love the idea of the optative. I wish we did more of it.

Daniel Levitin, a Professor of Psychology, Behavioural Neuroscience and Music at McGill University in Canada, is also keen that we do more daydreaming. He thinks that the 'mind-wandering mode' is responsible for our moments of greatest creativity and insight. It is when we are free associating that we make those seemingly random connections that end up solving our most intractable problems. He says this mode is also our neural reset button, to restore a sense of perspective when we are bogged down by multitasking. But it is interesting what happens when you invite people to daydream. One of my Ashridge colleagues John Neal often asks people to do a visioning exercise, where they have to close their eyes and imagine teeing-off on a golf course. The context is about future success and about the use of visualization in sports coaching. But when you ask the room to indicate whether any of them imagined a hole-in-one, no one puts their hand up. Why do we all imagine sub-optimally? Because we are not bold enough to dream big.

The exercise

For you, dreaming your own dreams, it is about taking off the blinkers. Your careful brain will be used to the habitual editing out of crazy options, but these might actually be the seeds of something promising. Creativity tools are often simple over-rides for this process, so that potential solutions are not discounted until the very final stage in the thinking process. So when you are dreaming big about your future, take the filters off. If you had all the time in the world ... ? If you had all the resources you would ever need ... ? If you did not care what people thought ... ? Answering these questions might well give you the germ of an idea and some really meaty obstacles to plan to overcome. Again, in our original future leaders research, many leaders wished they had known earlier that they could really do it. Lacking the confidence to push ahead, they had lost time and opportunity, because of this absence of self-belief.

For your leading, you need to widen out your gaze and dream for your organization too, in the same way. And to help suspend the filters of your colleagues until the very last minute. Optimism is one of Daniel Goleman's core emotional competencies. We love to follow leaders who give us hope and paint a picture of it for us. Not a foolishly optimistic one, perhaps – holes-in-one are quite rare. But a picture that rings true, like Shakespeare's famous speech by Henry V to the troops before the battle of Agincourt. Knowing how much veterans enjoy telling war stories, he talks about them sitting down to feast with their neighbours on a future St Crispin's Day and proudly showing off their Agincourt scars to everyone present. Of course, the battle will be costly, but it will be worth it.

We met reframing in the context of managing emotions. Reframing is fundamentally about silver linings: it is about relentlessly seeing the positive side of things. You may remember this is what Mark Twain's Tom Sawyer did when he had to whitewash Aunt Polly's fence. He reframed it so successfully as a privilege and a joy that his friends paid him to let them help. I like to befuddle students by starting all discussions of ethics with this question: do you exist? Crazy lady. But rather serious. Because we cannot actually prove that we do exist. We cannot prove that the world is real, because we cannot stand outside of it in order to see it properly. Many plots in movies and fiction centre around this theme, with the protagonist 'waking up' to realize that their previous reality was not real. So theoretically it could be that everything we experience is a figment of our imagination. Those religious traditions that believe in fate play a similar game, when they ask what the Divine means them to learn from whatever it is that has happened. It is a brilliant thought experiment when things go wrong, because you can ask yourself, if this has been created for me, what am I supposed to be getting out of it? This may be whimsy, but it is also useful, because it automatically reframes everything that happens to you as an opportunity.

So next time you are about to brief the team about the future, check that you are offering them hope. If you are not a glass half-full person, enlist the help of colleagues who are, to help keep team spirits up. And next time your team experiences a setback, set them a 'reframing' challenge. Give the person in your team who comes up with the best reframe a prize – perhaps a Jammie Dodger with a smiley face?

5 of Diamonds – initiative

The idea

Another of Daniel Goleman's core emotional competencies is initiative. It is about having a forwards drive that draws people to you and creates momentum and a sense of travel. People look to be led into a positive future of some kind, so showing initiative is a very pure form of leading. This is one of those competencies that does not sit comfortably with all personality types. Some people are happier to initiate than others. Sometimes this is generous, sometimes it is about control. Either way, if this is not a preference of yours you will still need to know how to exercise it skilfully when required.

The exercise

You could start limbering up with small steps. You could decide to make one proactive suggestion a day, be it where to go for lunch, how to solve a work problem, or what to cook for dinner. Do not be put off if your suggestions are not always pursued, just keep making offers until it feels more natural to do so. Then try to broaden this into other initiative taking, like offering to take responsibility for meeting actions or taking on the leadership of a work project. As you build your confidence and the confidence in you of those around you, you will feel braver about being more proactive in general. And as you are building your skill in this area, notice what other leaders around you do to demonstrate their initiative. When does this work well? When it does not, how could you do it better?

In many ways initiative is the opposite of our Jack of Diamonds, letting go, so you may want to practise toggling between these two exercises to test your ability both to diagnose what is required and to switch modes with ease.

4 of Diamonds – habits

The idea

Habits are vital for our day-to-day operating. The neural shortcuts they represent save us valuable processing time so that we can get on with our lives. As we deploy these heuristics, our mental maps are reinforced and the habits get stronger and even more effortless as time goes on. This also makes them extremely hard to shift.

In Charles Duhigg's book, *The Power of Habit*, he tells the famous story of Febreze, an odourless air freshener developed by Procter and Gamble in 1996. It was so brilliant that NASA used it to clean their shuttles when they returned from space. Yet it flopped as a consumer product. When the team looked carefully enough, they discovered that people were not using it because they had got so used to the bad smells around them there was no 'cue' to trigger usage. Further, if they did use it, there was no positive 'reward' – the bad smell simply disappeared. When they viewed hours of video of people cleaning their houses, they noticed that at the end of each chore or room, the cleaner had a ritual – a smile, or a pat of the bed, or a plumping of cushions, as they signed off from the activity. So they relaunched Febreze with a fragrance, and a commercial that showed a person cleaning a room then using Febreze for a celebratory and fragranced spritz when they were done. Cue, Routine, Reward. This in a nutshell is Duhigg's thesis – habits need all three; so, if you want to change a habit, you need to disrupt a step in this process.

Suppose you take sugar in your tea. This behaviour is so hardwired you do it on autopilot. Cue – kettle boils. Routine – line up the mug, the teabag, the sugar and the spoon. Reward – the first sip tastes perfect.

But what if you want to make your dentist happy or lose an inch off your waistline? It is terribly easy to respond automatically when you hear the kettle boil and absentmindedly stir in the sugar while you talk over your shoulder to someone. The first sip is so normal it is not until much later you remember you were supposed to have given up sugar. So the smart people physically move the sugar bowl, to upset the routine. While you are trying to locate it, you are more likely to remember that you put it away to avoid temptation and refrain from sugaring your tea. If you tend to scoff biscuits in meetings, you might remove the 'cue' by taking the plate of biscuits over to someone else's desk. If you reward yourself with wine at the end of a busy day and want to drink less, you may need to develop a different reward strategy, like extraordinary puddings, addictive box sets or an extravagant treat of some other kind. This 'substitution' is the reason so many ex-smokers turn to sweets, so do be careful you are not just replacing vice with vice.

You also need to remember that habits are supposed to be good – they are helpful ways to satisfy a need in the most efficient way possible. So you need to identify the underlying need they satisfy before you can change them permanently. And how long does it take to shift a habit? Phillippa Lally and her team found that it ranges from eighteen to 254 days, with the average time being sixty-six days. So at least two months, on average. Given that you will need extra processing power to cope with the neurological disruption you will be causing, you will need to be able to afford this extra energy over a sustained period of time. So pick your battles and do not do everything at once, but do not wait until you 'feel' like it. As Oliver Burkeman points out, we do not need to feel motivated to do something: we just have to do it. We should note our procrastinatory feelings and get on with it anyhow.

The exercise

Identify a habit you would like to shift. What is good about this habit? What is it helping you to do with the minimum of mental effort? Why do you want to change it? And do you feel fit and well enough to take on this change now? If not, come back to this exercise when you do. First, what is the cue that triggers this habit? Next, what routine ensues? Finally, what is the immediate reward at the end of the sequence? And which of these is most susceptible to interruption?

We looked at the sugar-in-tea example, where moving the sugar bowl was the neatest interruption. What equivalent might there be for you, to break the pattern and allow you to choose an alternative? And keep going – it may take a while for your replacement habit to form.

Here is a worked example for you. Say that one of your habits is always to proffer advice when you are asked for help, but you want to improve your coaching skills. Your cue is being asked a question, the routine is your answer, and the reward is that you feel helpful. In this case there is also a language trap, in that the whole point of deploying a question is to solicit an answer. So it is cued on both levels. In this instance, you have to work hard to interrupt your automatic answering of the question. One way to try this is to programme in an alternative response. Perhaps you could try always answering a question with a formula like 'say more'? This gives you thinking time, like moving the sugar bowl, so you can decide whether you want to answer the question or try a coaching question instead.

3 of Diamonds – missing person

The idea

There are lots of tools around for spotting gaps in teams or thinking processes: Meredith Belbin's team profiles, Edward de Bono's Six Thinking Hats, psychometrics like the Myers Briggs Type Indicator or any variation on the theme of diversity and range. My favourite is much simpler. It is a very neat exercise that the trainer Roger Greenaway uses, as part of his active reviewing process for team performance. It is called 'missing person' and works well for leaders as well as in a team context. The principle is a simple one. Imagine you had a colleague who was off today. Which is a shame, because had they been present, your team would have pulled an absolute blinder. Draw this missing person, as specifically as you can. Would they have big ears for all that excellent listening? Octopus tentacles for multitasking? Extra eyes to spot things you missed? It is a very neat way of identifying gaps without blaming the individuals who were part of the team today and to suggest areas for future development.

The exercise

In this context I would like to propose a variation. I do still want you to try to draw the person, because drawing uses a different part of your brain. This time, though, imagine you have an identical twin or a job-share colleague, whose presence completes you. Specifically, what do they do that complements your gifts and skills, either adding to them or compensating for your weaknesses? Developing this profile can flag your development needs but, more importantly, it tells you who you need to have in your team. Too many leaders recruit in their own image, when what you actually need is a team that represents between them the complete package.

2 of Diamonds – role models

The idea

The term 'role model' is bandied about so much that it has lost its power, but we have always learned instinctively through copying, ever since we were born. We are so used to doing so, that we are often unaware that we are imitating others and would tend to deny it. Marketers know this well, which is why they use celebrity endorsement and product placement. Mirroring in body language; trends in speech patterns or vocabulary; and the copying of the dress and accessories of those we admire socially, are other common examples of this phenomenon. Nowhere more so than in the workplace, when we are simultaneously trying to learn, to fit in, and to impress. This makes it highly likely we will end up copying the high-status people around us, consciously or not. Which is why achieving diversity in all its guises is so crucially important at board level.

The exercise

Appoint some role models. Deliberately selecting your role models is a good way to avoid copying the wrong ones by default. You should have several of them, for various aspects of your life and career. Some you may not wish to know that they are your role models, some you may wish to acquire formally as mentors. Either way, hedge your bets: internal career mentors are useful until they fall out of favour and take you down with them.

At the same time, return the favour. Who is following you and why? Who might you be a role model for, and can you take care to behave like one? You may have a junior colleague that you admire – could they be your upward mentor, to keep you in touch with their generation or their particular perspective? If there is no obvious candidate in your own organization, offer to mentor within the sector – you will learn as much as they will, and it is a good way to practise your core skills.

Chapter 7

Clubs

Your physical impact

The club in a pack of cards reminds me of those cartoons about cavemen, who carried clubs around for seeing off the odd anachronistic dinosaur. So I have grouped under this suit those practices and exercises that are about optimizing your physical impact. Some of them focus on 'the meat' – are you healthy, rested and well, and is the way you are living your life sustainable? And some of them – also physical – are more concerned with how you actually show up in person on the day. Are you clear about your exercise of power and control? Do you convey impact and the right kind of image and status for the job in hand? And how multi-channel is this, in the days of social media and a personal brand that can be destroyed through one careless tweet? Use the table below to self-score as you read through the section.

Table 4 Clubs

Clubs		RAG	Next chance to practise
A♣	Work–Life Balance		
K♣	Sleep		
Q♣	Fuel		
J♣	Personal Brand		
10♣	Change		
9♣	Reading Cultures		
8♣	Power		
7♣	Control		
6♣	Gravitas		
5♣	Posture		
4♣	Sumptuary Law		
3♣	Colours		
2♣	Social Media		

Ace of Clubs – work–life balance

The idea

Work–life balance? The phrase gives itself away. As a partner at Deloitte once told a group of us young things, 'it's in that order'. We know this, because if someone asks us how we are, we say 'Busy!' in a slightly manic way, as though that is the right answer. There are lots of great tools out there for auditing your life choices and how you apportion your time. I think the best I have found is the Balance Matrix, invented by the author Lauren Bacon, that juxtaposes energy and agenda.

She distinguishes between things that drain you and are on someone else's agenda (drudgery) and things that energize you and are on your agenda (fun and purpose). You still have to earn a living, though, but hopefully much of your work, while it is not directly in service of your own agenda, is nonetheless energizing (rewarding work). Brace yourself, though, for 'tasks' which further your own agenda but feel tedious - at least the 'fun and purpose' stuff fuels you for them.

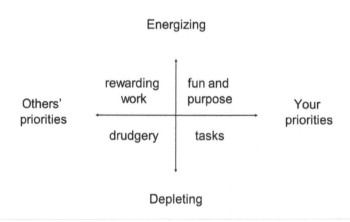

Figure 4 The balance matrix

The exercise

How can you use this matrix in practice? First, try to map your diary on to it. How well are you already managing to balance your time? I would guess that the fun and purpose box is a bit squeezed out by the other three. So how can you grow this bit of your world? Well, tasks have to be done, but can you outsource them at all? Drudgery, too. Could you delegate any of these activities? And can you transform even the rewarding work into fun and purpose by getting clearer about how serving your organization's agenda also serves yours? In all 3 of these quadrants, there is an opportunity to transform activities into purposeful opportunities for learning. Can you use a boring meeting as an apprentice piece to practise your listening skills? Can you cheer your commute, the school run, or your housework, with carefully chosen audio books and TED talks? And how can you find more opportunities to smuggle fun and purpose into your day job? Keep a track of this with post-it notes. How many of your activities have you managed to sneak into your energizing/my agenda box this month?

King of Clubs – sleep

The idea

If you were to pause your next team meeting and ask everyone to line up in order of the amount of sleep they had last night, you would be shocked at how badly they are all sleeping. Sometimes this is because of young children, but more often than not it is because of stress. In one of their periodic 'bedroom' surveys, Ashridge found that managers spend fewer than seven hours asleep at night, and this decreases as seniority increases. Match this up with a long-day no-lunch culture and this becomes an extremely alarming statistic. As the sleep expert Vicki Culpin puts it, seventeen hours of sustained wakefulness has been shown to result in changes in behaviour equivalent to drinking two glasses of wine. In most countries people who have drunk this much are not allowed to drive or operate machinery, yet their equivalents are at the helm of some of our largest companies, making really scary decisions, every single day.

Of the 340 managers surveyed, over 80 per cent reported waking up at least once during the night, taking increasing lengths of time to fall back to sleep in line with seniority. The CEOs in the sample took 30 minutes to fall back to sleep each time and 72 per cent of all managers polled said they routinely found it difficult to concentrate on tasks because of lack of sleep. Given that a reduction in sleep by only 1.5 hours per night for one night alone can result in a decrease in daytime alertness by 32 per cent, a team with three insomniac managers is functioning the equivalent of a man down. Good quality sleep is also necessary to build memories, so persistent insomnia has an increasingly negative effect on recall and performance over time. These statistics should seriously alarm boards and shareholders, and those responsible for analysing corporate risk, decision-making and executive performance.

Research suggests that the brain's executive function is best topped up through sleep, so if your sleep is deficient, you start each day behind. The executive function is how we self-regulate. Operating like the brain's PA, it organizes our behaviour, regulating and monitoring it in response to the environment, and it controls our actions and emotions. The executive function helps the brain to cope with complexity, creativity and problem-solving, and controls inhibition and the ability to assess risk. When we use willpower, energy is used up, as reflected in increased heart-rate variability and a reduction in blood glucose levels. These levels need to be topped up for us to continue to function well and, while food, water, self-esteem and distraction can help, rest and sleep are the key levers.

Ashridge's findings on sleep and self-regulation paint a gloomy picture and other sleep studies tend to agree. If managers have effortful jobs and work long days, over time their ability to make good decisions will simply drain away, as will their ability either to notice or to stop it from happening. And it is worsened by the everyday efforts all managers make that require willpower: coping with difficult colleagues, handling complaints, biting your tongue, being patient and resisting temptation.

There are various things you can do to top-up during a stressful day. Eating lunch, drinking water and taking a walk round the block between meetings. Or eating bananas, going to the gym and improving your self-esteem through altruistic acts. Companies can also help by taking this issue more seriously. After all, getting it right looks like it would seriously improve corporate performance. If your employees are working late and taking work home, you need to re-evaluate their workload, in case the cost of bad decision-making outweighs any savings you have made by downsizing.

As Arianna Huffington puts it, it is time we slept our way to the top. She also thinks we should switch off. In her book, *The Sleep Revolution*, she recommends avoiding the kind of blue light that our gadgets emit for at least 30 minutes before bed. She is an advocate of bedtime meditation, breathing exercises and counting your blessings, which is known to help you sleep better. Bizarrely, research by Liu and team showed that drinking tart cherry juice twice a day also helps boost sleep.

And Culpin has this advice for wakeful managers. Try to avoid alcohol, caffeine and fatty, spicy or sugary foods 4–6 hours before bedtime. Exercise regularly, but not directly before you go to sleep. Keep your bedroom well ventilated, temperate, dark and quiet. Reserve it for sleeping and try a light snack like a banana or warm milk before turning in. We have already met my favourite piece of advice about insomnia: just try extremely hard to keep your eyes open. It works every time.

The exercise

Keep a sleep diary for a week. You can do this by journaling, or if you have a smartphone or wearable tech you could try a sleep app. What do you notice? How could you improve your sleep? Looking at the suggestions above, which could you try, and what will you do differently tonight?

Queen of Clubs – fuel

The idea

The Romans had a term for it: *mens sana in corpore sano* – a healthy mind in a healthy body. Too many leaders are so busy tackling the intellectual challenges of their roles that many of them neglect their ability to cope with the physical challenges of their roles. Of course, paying attention to what you eat, how healthy you are and how well you sleep are the obvious priorities. However, the best insight into this area that I have found came from my colleague Angela Muir, when she studied ego depletion for her masters under Chris Dewberry at Birkbeck. She explains the concept as being about your 'battery', and about the amount of willpower you have from day to day. Specifically, it is about the capacity of the executive function, which we have already met. This 'grown-up' in your head is the one who helps you to function well by paying attention, making decisions, fielding novelty, planning the future and overriding unhelpful impulses. The theory is that we function like a battery in this area. All things being well, we start each day refreshed and fully charged. As the day progresses, our energy ebbs away, being particularly depleted by effortful activity carried out by the executive function. As Caroline Webb argues in her book, *How to Have a Good Day*, it is when this deliberate part of our brain wearies that our subconscious takes over. This is just our brain trying to help by lightening the load, but it makes us vulnerable to auto-pilot reactions that may not fit the bill.

There is currently a storm brewing as academics worldwide fight about whether or not the various measures adopted to test the concept of ego depletion are robust or stable. While the science catches up, I would like you to consider this as a thought experiment, because of its link with more established thinking on cognitive overload, which we have already discussed in considering attention.

The exercise

Let us think of all the things that are absolutely guaranteed to drain your energy flat out of you. These are your Harry Potter-style Dementors: bad weather, transport glitches, annoying people, pointless meetings, IT breakdowns, anything that renders you incoherent with rage, or instantly punctures your mood. Lots of these are not in your gift, but many of them appear predictably throughout the day, week in, week out. Looking at your diary, can you predict any of them right now?

Rather than letting fate hit you, why not schedule in some contingency action instead. These are your 'whiskers on kittens', in homage to Julie Andrews' famous ditty from the musical *The Sound of Music*. Anything that makes you smile, restores your balance, cheers you up or calms you down. There are some generics that we know boost mood: rest, water, bananas, flattery, laughter, singing, music, dancing, beauty, altruism, exercise, outdoors, mindfulness, meditation, prayer, friends, nurture, cat videos (!). But what else gives you joy, peace and perspective? Look at your diary and be realistic about which days in the weeks to come are most likely to feature high levels of Dementor activity. Rather than giving into it, plan now which items from your kittens list you could mobilize in your own defence. A draining day of sales calls? Book in a call to your best friend half-way through, or reward yourself at the end of the day with a takeaway and a favourite movie.

You might also want to have a design for your perfect day in your back pocket, for times when you are preparing for a particularly important meeting, speech or interview. Do you know what you would need to lay on for yourself to feel refreshed, relaxed, at peace and full of energy? Keep a list of all the things that help, so you can deploy them when you cannot think straight but need rescuing. They might not always be in your gift, but many of them can be contrived and they will act as an immediate antidote to anything that is trying your mood. One client always chooses outrageous flattery as her screen unlock, so that many times a day she is typing 'hellocleverclogs' or something similar. And on difficult days, try to eat foods that will boost your energy and not consume it. Go easy on treating yourself with pizza and a large glass of wine, in case the reward itself becomes your next problem.

Jack of Clubs – personal brand

The idea

The more senior you become, the more necessarily remote you are. Partly because you will have diminishing opportunities for 1:1 time with your staff, and partly because you will physically be out of the office a lot more, managing external stakeholders. This means that perception becomes more influential than reality, because so few people have direct sight of you as you really are in all your guises. This is normal and wholly taken for granted, but it has a downside. This is because the Core Group effect gets riskier the less visible you become and followers fill gaps with conjecture and guesswork. So leaders need to make it as easy as possible for their default settings to be visible. You need to become a master at managing how you are perceived. Is everyone clear what you stand for, what your priorities are, and what you want them to do if they are unclear?

One way to address this is through the idea of personal branding, because what every leader really needs is a strong brand signature. Professional branding is a constantly evolving field, accelerating now with the advent of social media, rendering many of the older branding models obsolete. Originally, branding cattle was a way of showing ownership; the branding of goods and services is similarly about establishing a common association between potentially disparate things. In taking this notion forward, marketers these days pay particular attention to brand essence, or what it is that unites these products, beyond the physical logo and colours that formally identify them. So brand is about a promise and about a relationship. If you buy brand x, you will always get benefits y and z. This generates customer loyalty over time, which boosts sales and profits. This concept is very relevant for leaders, because it is about high-level messaging and the ability to convey trust through a simple brand signature.

I once had the pleasure of teaching some leaders from Trinity House, the General Lighthouse Authority, which is the body responsible for all the lighthouses in England and Wales. They told me that there is a special code book that tells you the light signature for each one, so that even if you had no idea where you were on the map, you could find out by consulting the code book. I love this idea of a 'flash pattern', and it is exactly what I mean by the leader's brand signature, because a leader should seek to be as consistent as a lighthouse in the messages they send out.

The exercise
You already have a brand, so the first step is to tune into it, then decide whether or not it serves you. Start by emailing ten people you know to ask them for three words that they feel best sum you up. Compare these to see if any themes emerge. If you can, ask them to provide examples where these words are evidenced, as a way of understanding what is meant by them and what signals you are sending out. You can also

validate your words if you are feeling brave, by seeking first impression words from people you have just met, next time you are on a course or in some other context where this is a safe thing to ask. Looking at these words, do you like them? Do they feel true? Are they useful? If any of them do not feel appropriate, how could you alter the signals you send out to change the message that is being received?

For instance, one of my words was 'quick'. The person giving it to me explained that this was sometimes very positive, as in quick-witted. But that sometimes I was too quick – quick to judge; so quick in speaking it was hard to hear me; and so quick to reply to questions it looked like I was not listening well. This was a really helpful reminder that an intellectual strength was an interpersonal weakness in some contexts, and that I should rein it in where it would be a barrier to others. And how do you make adjustments like this? By using pauses, doing more active listening, and checking back with questioners before responding to them. I still do not always get it right, but it was very useful feedback.

Commercial brands are tested and strengthened by challenges to them, and companies know that a complaint is really an opportunity to convert a customer into a long-term brand-fan if the complaint is dealt with well. So, like your character more generally, the challenges you face as a leader will reinforce your brand, or force you to change it. Being clearer about your flash pattern also gives you a brand anchor, for when you need to deliberately reinforce it, review it, or check your decision-making against it. If anything ever happens that makes your organization worried, choose an opportunity to prove your brand to them in public. Like ships in a storm, they will automatically seek out the nearest lighthouse when the weather worsens and will be reassured by your steady light.

10 of Clubs – change

The idea

There is a brilliant sign in a pub somewhere in mid-Wales, above a small dish. It says, 'if you fear change, leave it here'. While change is normal, it can feel like loss, or at least about having to make a big effort to establish a new habit. So it is not surprising that many of us struggle with it, because it requires a lot of energy from us.

I used to do change management for a living, so I have met a whole range of change models: houses, steps, grids, circles, transitions, pathways – as many models as there are gurus and consulting firms to sell them. I have not yet met one that was not based on the Kübler-Ross grief curve. You may know this model, which is about the range of emotions typically experienced on the death of a loved one. It was devised by Swiss psychiatrist Elisabeth Kübler-Ross in 1969, inspired by her work with the terminally ill, through research on death and those faced with it at the University of Chicago medical school. The five stages are expressed as denial, anger, bargaining, depression and acceptance, and are often drawn as a u-shaped curve. She later extended her work to include any form of personal loss, such as job loss, loss of freedom, relationship break-up or major illness, although in later life she conceded that not all experiences follow such a linear grief path.

I was rather suspicious about the connection between grief and change, until I started doing an exercise about change that asks people to pair up, change three things about their appearance and see if their partner can spot them. Every single time I have run this exercise, every single person starts by losing something – a ring, a watch, a tie, a shoe – their instinct is to take something off. It is only after a few iterations of this exercise that people start adding things and borrowing things; copying, sharing and experimenting; all the kinds of positive behaviours that you really want during times of change. And the process of initially rejecting, then wrestling with, then integrating, new data is how we learn anything new in any case.

So given the assumption of loss, helping others in transition is about establishing for each of them what they stand to gain, so they feel it is worth making the effort. You might have to work quite hard to identify something, but you will be able to do so. You can practise this by combining this competence with the one relating to optimism and by searching out silver linings. Often this is about development opportunities for staff, the opportunity to impress key influencers, or a way to learn valuable CV skills. Looking back, which changes have you most dreaded and, with the benefit of hindsight, what did you learn from them that has stood you in good stead? How might this perspective help you to help others? And if you want to keep yourself limber, make small changes every day. Drive a new way to work. Walk a new route round the office. Have something different for lunch. Sit in a new spot at meetings. Use a new pen. Anything to disrupt your patterns so you know you can do it when it really matters.

The exercise
When you next encounter resistance to any change you are trying to implement – major or minor – here is a handy tool you can deploy. At Deloitte, we used to work with clients implementing change programmes to map people on a 'resistance wheel' around these three variables – lack

Figure 5 The resistance wheel

of: Understanding, Skills or Motivation. Of course this was a bit basic, but it remains a useful rule of thumb if you do not use it pejoratively.

1   Understanding
    A sense that you are not understood is theoretically an easy problem to solve. If people are not responding to you in the way you intend, perhaps they genuinely do not see what you see. And, writ large, this is why so much time is spent in organizations on internal communications initiatives. So can you slow down, rewind and listen? Can you figure out what it is in your head that makes this a no-brainer for you that they cannot see yet? What else could you do to improve their understanding about this issue?

2   Skills
    Immortalized in the Star Trek movie *The Undiscovered Country*, there is a story about the origins of the word 'sabotage'. Valeris tells Uhura and Chekov that '400 years ago' on planet Earth, when the workers felt threatened by industrialization, they threw their wooden clogs – sabots – into the machines to stop them working. This is exactly why so many cups of coffee were accidentally spilled on keyboards to disable them, when secretaries were miraculously supposed to transfer their skills from typewriters to computers with no training and feared for their jobs if their lack of ability to do so was discovered. So before you react to distracting behaviour, check it is not actually a cry for help. If there is a skills gap, it is relatively straightforward to address it through coaching, mentoring, training or transitioning.

3   Motivation
    While there are ready-made strategies to address gaps in understanding and skill through communication and training, motivation is a tougher nut to crack. It certainly helps to start by acknowledging this gap and by finding ways for people to participate. But if you have managed your Gallup 12 scores up and there is still a problem, what do you do? If I had a silver bullet, I would give it to you. Actually, I do. It is called love. Everyone is supremely motivated to do the things they love, for the people they love. The bare truth is that in many organizations we ask people to do pretty rubbish things, for no good reason and we are not all that nice to them about it. So before you bust

a gut coming up with cunning wheezes, ask them why they work and why they do this job in particular. If you are feeling brave, ask them what they love. Then ask them where they want to go next. Finally, be honest. Explain why this change will ultimately help them meet their goals. And if it will not, say so and explain why you are asking them to do it anyway. And if they say no, you have to respect that and work on plan B. Not everyone feels like you do about their job and we all have different ways of making meaning about our occupation. Brilliant leaders do seem to be able to find some up-side for even the most die-hard refusenik, so do not be afraid to take advice from wiser heads when you are up against it. Because 'taking people with you' - all of them, not just the easy ones - is what leading is really all about.

9 of Clubs – reading culture

The idea

In the US, Walmart famously has the Walmart Cheer to galvanize the workers. In the UK, Tesco has the 4 o'clock rumble, where staff down tools and take to the aisles, pulling forward produce from the back of the shelves for the next wave of shoppers. As in poker, these cultural 'tells' often say more about a company's values than can the most carefully crafted piece of webpage copy. And honing your ability to pick up these signals will improve your organizational empathy, a key emotional competence.

When my colleague wanted to buy a bike, he took to hanging out with the smokers where groups of couriers congregate. They are bike experts, because they depend on them for their work. However, they are also experts in organizational mood. Want to know how your competitors are doing? Ask the couriers who deliver to them. Is the reception busy and buzzing? Who is signing in to the visitors' book, or waiting in reception? How do the staff behave, and are the receptionists rude about the organization when no 'insiders' are in earshot? Busy people have grown up learning by instinctively absorbing environmental signals. So what is your company leaking? Does it undermine your 'inside-out' branding and give away what is really going on?

I used to work for the Church Commissioners on Millbank in London. While I was there, we reorganized in an attempt to streamline the national structures. Our merger partner was the huge machine that is the General Synod office in Church House. One interesting cultural artefact that summed up the nature of the challenge was the additional day's holiday we were each awarded every year: for Synod, Ascension Day, for the Commissioners, the Queen's Birthday. Church versus State, and who should win? And when I worked for Deloitte, they made a huge effort to portray themselves as 'hip' to attract the pony-tailed dot-com generation. When the order was given to move to dress-down Fridays, two memos came out. One, from the Consulting practice, said: 'please don't wear anything to the office in which you'd be ashamed to meet a client'. The guidance from the Audit firm ran to several pages, detailing acceptable brands and generating new rules like avoiding 'patch pockets', these being considered less formal than tailored ones on a 'smart casual' trouser.

Other cultural tells include the code book issued by Deloitte to help us decipher the forest of acronyms deployed in the MOD, which had presumably been intended to fox the eavesdropping Russians in the days of the Cold War. In the late 1990s, you could tell there was trouble with the new telecoms strategy at Marconi, when so many office walls still boasted pictures of military hardware. And when I moved to Ashridge, I met a whole range of customer-first rules, like reserving the bananas for participants and not eating lunch until 1.15 p.m. so they could have first pick.

The exercise

Next time you meet a courier or a delivery man, or the taxi driver who takes your competitors to the airport, ask them lots of questions. Next time you visit an office, switch your radar on and see what you can pick up – what sense of the culture are you getting and what specifically gives it away? Take a look around your own organization – what do people really believe about the company? Because they will be giving it away in how they choose to act, particularly in the case of those small things that normally do not matter. What could you do to deliberately communicate the kind of culture you want around you?

8 of Clubs – power

The idea

There is a huge literature on power in the fields of sociology, psychology and political theory. Practically speaking, the models of power that are the most useful are those that tell you how to get more of it. So I like the classic model established by John R. P. French and Bertram Raven in 1959, as embroidered over the years by successive Ashridge faculty. It may not be the most accurate or nuanced account of power, but it is the most useful I have found.

My version of the model establishes three sets of power bases: role power, convening power and personal power. Role power, often called legitimate or position power, is about your role or job title. And this job gives you two levers, the power to reward and the power to coerce. This power includes your ability to deploy resources and attaches to you while you occupy the role. It is a property of the job, so it stays with it if you move on. This is why so many leaders who used to rely on their official position to make them feel powerful struggle in retirement and decorate the boards of charities to recover a semblance of this lost power. Convening power, for me, is your ability to borrow power, typically from what you know (information) and who you know (networks). Thanks to the internet, whole new industries have now emerged to empower us through Google and other search engines; Wikipedia and websites; and the networks created by social media. The third power base is your personal power, the only one of the three that is both owned and immediate, because it is yours to use now and yours to keep forever. This power comprises your personality and your expertise, both again susceptible to improvement to help you empower yourself.

The exercise

Like a battery, power is latent and lies passive until it is switched on. Influence is power applied, power deployed, power delivered; so influence is most often about relative power. Thinking about a situation in which you wish you had more influence, where is the imbalance in power? How could you make yourself feel more powerful in this situation? Using French and Raven's categories, map the other party's imagined power against yours. Where are there imbalances? Is there anything inherent in your role that allows you to offer rewards or threaten coercion? What is in it for them, or is there a favour they owe you? Could you use your network or the internet to find out more about the person you want to influence? Is there someone in your network that they always listen to, who you could send on your behalf? Or is there information you could get for them that they would welcome? Could you use your personality more skilfully with them? How could you apply or improve your expertise more powerfully in this situation?

As a quick tip for a power-boost, you might consider power priming. Research carried out by Lammers and Galinsky suggests that in an interview or important meeting, you will come across as more persuasive if you have recalled immediately beforehand a time when you have felt powerful. So, when you are waiting in the lobby, type yourself an email or text about all the times in your life when you have been absolutely fabulous. Or at least call these occasions to mind as you travel up in the lift.

7 of Clubs – control

The idea

One of the psychometric instruments we use at Ashridge measures control. Specifically, how much of it managers want and how much of it they display. You will not be surprised to hear that the norm data shows managers to be higher than average on the amount of control they want, and that they tend to want to be controlled rather less. So if you are reading this, it is likely you have a preference for control and do not generally like ceding control to others.

The exercise

Next time you feel control slipping away when plans change, perhaps you could try adjusting your sphere of control. On one facilitation course I attended, each group had to build a see-saw. This was to illustrate the central message of the workshop. It worked, because I can proudly tell you now that Process was the fulcrum to balance Task and

People. Task, People, Process. And that is it, really – you can always control one of them, even if it is just you. And because all work is a balance between task, people and process, if you are thwarted on any of them, you can shift your attention to the one that you can influence instead.

Maybe a task deadline has changed. Could you instead influence the scope or quality of the task, or negotiate about the time commitment of the people involved? Or perhaps someone has let you down. If they are no longer available, could you renegotiate the deadline or the extent of the job they were to do for you? Could you go back to the person who wants the job done and clarify the process so you can find a good replacement? Or maybe the report you thought you were writing now needs to include a whole range of analysis you had not factored in. Can you get the deadline extended, or lobby for more help? It is hard to become instantly flexible in the face of change, but practising resource-fulness about influence able variables will help you over time to see possibility rather than just pain.

6 of Clubs – gravitas

The idea
One of the most elusive properties of seniority seems to be gravitas. But having hung out with a lot of leaders, I think I have nailed it for you: it is essentially about supply and demand. In general, 'wise' people seem to say less, so what they do say seems more valuable and the result of deep thought. They might actually have been planning their weekend in all that silence, but by the time they speak, we are agog and hanging on to every word.

The exercise
Next time you need to dial up your gravitas, dial down the amount you contribute. If you already have a preference for introversion, you are well ahead of the game. Otherwise, ration yourself in meetings by writing down your interjections rather than saying them. If your points are not made by others during the meeting, you will then be able to offer a timely reminder or a devastating summary. There is nothing

more eye-catching than a well-chosen 'we have missed something vital' or 'it seems to me that we face three key challenges'.

If you are trying to get into the zone, watch the Queen. Everything seems to slow down around her. Powerful people seem to be able to slow down time and to create space around them. As well as taking time and taking space, you might want to sit more strategically in meetings: opposite or diagonally to the Chair to influence them, beside the Chair to influence others. And ask questions, because questions make people think. And if you make people think, they think you are wise.

5 of Clubs – posture

The idea

Have you ever noticed how distinctive a walk is? You can recognize a friend coming towards you in the distance, long before you can see their face. Our bodies have a signature already. The acting profession has had to get expert at replicating body signatures, particularly in stage acting, when the audience may not be able to see every detail of your face. Especially for plays that have a small cast, playing the full range of characters. How do you change from being a child to being an old lady? You do it partly through costume, but mainly through your body. Equally, switching from being a servant to playing the king requires a physical adjustment, to signal to the audience that you are believable in this new role. There are lessons we can learn about communication from these technical skills. At the extremes, if you are playing a low status character, you minimize. You take up less space, you look and sound more tentative, and you are anxious to please. In contrast, if you watch actors playing royalty or statesmen, they take up a lot of space. They slow everything right down and they talk in a deliberate and measured way. If you are watching a movie or programme where costume does not give it away, try turning the volume down so you can watch the physical interactions. You will be able to guess status, power and affiliation from what you observe. Or pause on the balcony above your next conference to watch how people behave.

We like to imagine that our words outweigh our physicality. Indeed, it is rather important that we do not let unconscious bias about physical attributes fool us into discriminatory behaviour. However, how you choose to carry yourself is already sending out a message and you can vary this message by varying how you physically show up. Let us focus specifically on how you can display confident behaviours. Because if you behave confidently, you will be received confidently, creating a virtuous circle that will end up giving you more confidence.

Harvard's Amy Cuddy is the guru on this. Her TED Talk has been viewed by over 34 million people and is in their all-time top 20. She has written a book called *Presence* to unpack her ideas. In a nutshell, her research shows that humans (and some other species) automatically hold up their arms in triumph when they win a race or a competition of some kind. Even if they are blind. And she has found that if you adopt this posture before an event, with your arms in a 'V' and your chin raised, it raises testosterone and lowers cortisol. The reverse happens if you hunch up checking emails on your phone, because this is a lower status posture. She shows that how we hold our bodies shifts our mood, so we should 'fake it until we become it' if we are ever feeling at a disadvantage. Luckily, power-posing is the kind of activity you can do in the washroom before you sally forth.

The important thing about any body language you adopt is that it must be consistent with your words and your tone. There is no point showing up all-powerful if you cannot then get the words out. And you may recall the cartoon of a furious person, brows like thunder and arms crossed, biting out 'I'm fine'. We know we believe the body language and the tone over the words every time. A famous paper, published in 1976 in the journal *Nature* by McGurk and MacDonald, explains this, through the McGurk effect. They discovered that if you played a video of a person making one sound while dubbing over it a different sound, the visual data trumps the auditory data and overrides it. This is a version of the oft-quoted research by Albert Mehrabian, about the relative impact of verbal and non-verbal messages in inter-personal communication. His contemporaneous research also suggested that we get most of our clues about the emotional intent behind someone's words from non-verbal cues. So if you say confident things without looking confident, they will doubt you, because the signals are inconsistent.

The exercise

One quick trick on this? If you stand up for phonecalls you will have more impact.

As you wait for your next meeting or to give a presentation, build yourself up from your feet to your head, distributing your weight evenly and standing tall. Keeping your feet pointing straight forward will help keep your body straight, which makes you appear 'straight-forward' to others. Notice your knees and hips, and how your torso and shoulders are positioned. Relax your elbows, and hold your chin a little higher than you might normally do. Breathe from your diaphragm not your shoulders, and when you are nervous just listen to your breathing, which will calm you down. Smile, take in the room, and breathe out.

And, at your next meeting or work event, tune into the body language playing out around you. What do you notice?

4 of Clubs – sumptuary law

The idea

Have you ever wondered how on earth Cinderella got admitted to the ball without an invitation? If you have seen a formal court dress in a museum you will have seen why it was so very necessary that the fairy godmother made a decent effort on that gown. In the days before you could google people, one of the only ways to tell whether a stranger was the 'right' sort of person or not was by how they dressed. And if you wore court dress, you were clearly the right sort of person. This is called 'sumptuary law' and has ancient roots. In Rome, only the Emperor or the senators were permitted to wear purple, because the dye used to create Tyrian purple was so highly prized. Similarly, in China, only the Emperor could wear yellow. Elizabeth I was keen on sumptuary law and hers were very specific – for example, see Table 5 on the matter of fur, as on 15 June 1574.

Over the years, sumptuary laws have been used to reinforce social hierarchies, so they are no longer officially popular. Unofficially, they run rampant. Green wellies? Red trousers? Pearls? Nike trainers?

Table 5 The wearing of fur

Fur	Only to be worn by:
Sable	King, Queen, King's mother, children, brethren and sisters, uncles and aunts; dukes, marquises and earls; those of the Garter
Black civet, lynx	dukes, marquises, earls and their children; viscounts, barons and knights being companions of the Garter; or any person being of the Privy Council
Leopard	barons' sons, knights and gentlemen attendant upon her majesty; ambassadors
Grey furs except pine-marten and civet	men worth £100 a year; son of a knight
Black furs except civet	the Lord Chancellor, Treasurer, President of the Council, Privy Seal
Pine-marten, grey civet, lambskin	son and heir apparent of a man whose business is worth 300 marks a year and men whose household expense is £40 a year

Hoodies? Burberry? Not to mention subtle and local customs to do with cufflinks, watches and rings; the wearing of 'old school' ties, designer brands, or trophy accessories.

You have already heard my cufflinks story, but here is one about the BBC. When they were being the most creative organization in the world, a group of staff attended a course at Ashridge. We talked about status, which of course does not feature in such a flat and democratic organization. I ventured to suggest that the herding effect of office dress tends to feature at every level of the organization. They did admit that, having been casual all the way up, their seriously senior types reverted to suits at the top and stopped carrying backpacks. Then they looked at each other. The dress code for the course was 'business casual'. Every single man there was wearing a polo shirt, cargo shorts, Birkenstock sandals and a Storm watch. Without exception. And the (few) ladies present were dressed rather similarly. Nobody had conferred on a packing list, they had just all shown up dressed identically. What had made them gravitate towards these particular brands?

A BBC alpha male had started the trend, once, and invisibly they had all followed suit. They were mortified of course.

Lest you think this is just about style, the UK's Social Mobility Commission thinks it has real impact on career access. In their July 2016 report, *Socio-Economic Diversity in Life Sciences and Investment Banking*, they flagged the 'brown shoes' issue. Have you ever heard the saying 'never brown in town?' Apparently candidates are not getting City jobs because they wear brown shoes to interview. Remember, if Cinderella had got the dress code wrong, she would not have met her handsome prince, either.

The exercise

What games are being played around status and dress in your workplace and sector? Remember, if you are not playing the status-dressing game, you are playing the 'I'm not playing' game. Either way, points can mean prizes. Should you ever wish to bump up your status for a particular meeting or occasion, there are some tried-and-tested ways to do so. It used to be about swords and medals; now it tends to be about the things in Table 6. You get one 'point' for each; and should aim for around nine in a professional context.

Just a few explanatory notes. Those of you reading this who do not like shaving or do not wear make-up might feel judged by this list. Worry not – there are no compulsory items on the list, rather it is accumulative. You can heighten your status by adding points, as long as you calibrate with 'local' levels and do not overdo it. We have all seen what it looks like when people overdress, so the rule is to match your context and go 'one up' to signal status if you need to (e.g. in a presentation or job interview). It is all about dressing appropriately for your context, so that you enable people to respond to you in the right way. Men have slightly fewer options, so may need to indulge in power accessories instead (the 'right' pen or smartphone for your context). Because men cannot even-out skin tone with make-up, they need to be particularly careful about wearing a flattering colour close to the face.

Now that you have seen this list, you will have enormous fun trying to identify the power games that are already played around dress, brands and accessories in your working environment. It is always interesting

Table 6 Points

Ladies	Gentlemen
Make-up	Clean-shaven/neatly trimmed facial hair
Ringed fingers	Ringed fingers (max. 2 – wedding and signet)
Jacket	Jacket
Scarf	Tie
Brooch or decoration	Pocket square (handkerchief in breast pocket)
Watch	Watch
Earrings	Cufflinks
Necklace	Formal collar (not collarless or buttondown)
Bracelet	Shirt of the right weight – twofold 100% cotton
Shoes – smart/decorative	Polished shoes – leather soled
Colour (1 point for each, up to 3)	Colour (1 point for each, up to 3)
Manicured hands	Neat hands (unbitten nails)
Quality hosiery	Quality socks
Belt	Belt
Spectacles	Spectacles
Hat or visible hair decoration	Hat or groomed hair
Handbag	Waistcoat or smart briefcase accessory

to see the level of agreement in a room if you ask people to draw an archetypal 'senior person' in their organization – we all know the rules instinctively, even if we do not know that we do, or do not choose to follow them.

3 of Clubs – colours

The idea

Have you had your colours done? The most well-known systems are probably Colour Me Beautiful, House of Colour and Colour Affects, but there are hundreds of variations on this theme. Luckily, they are all based on the same core theory. And just to cheer you up about how terribly robust it all is, it is based on Aristotle. He originally identified blue and yellow as the universal core of colour, because blue is the first colour to appear out of darkness and yellow is the first colour to appear out of light. This is why the vast darkness of space looks to us like blue sky and the blinding white light of the sun looks like yellow. And whether you suit blue or yellow will determine which set of shades will normally suit you. These then split out into a clear or a muted version of the palette – bright colours or muddy ones.

Nowadays all the painstaking work done on colour wheels and colour families by Rittell, Goethe and the Bauhaus school has been monetized by the branding and design industries, for interior decoration and to dress actors so they convey a particular set of messages. You can be cynical about this and write it off as 1980s claptrap, or you can just save yourself a fortune and get your colours done. It will make you easier on the eye and it saves you time when shopping or selecting clothes to wear. It also stops you wasting money on clothes that make you look ill. I can now write off, entire shops or ranges on the basis of my ideal colour palette. I am not that bothered whether it is the absolute truth or not, but it means that everything I have goes with everything else and generally makes me look well. When I do go off-piste and snag myself a lilac bargain, everyone just asks me if I am getting enough sleep.

The exercise

You can do it yourself if you have good light at home. Hold up first something yellow, then something blue against your face. Look carefully at the effect each has on your eyes, hair and skin tone in particular. When you know which you are, find bright and muddy versions of warm or cool colours and do the same. Red is neutral, but cools will suit the kind of red that has more blue in it (mulberries and purples) while warms will prefer a red that is more terracotta or russet. If you can get a colour consultant to help, it is worth the investment, because of the extra tips you can pick up. But picking any palette and sticking to it will ensure you always look well-matched. As a rule of thumb, 'blues' suit silver and 'yellows' suit gold. Few people really suit black.

What colours mean is relative, because it depends very much on culture and context. But in a Western work setting there are some traditional norms you might care to follow when selecting your outfit. For business: black, grey and navy. For trust: blue. For creativity: green. For calm: purple. For confidence: red or pink. For energy and optimism: yellow or orange. If this is a one-off meeting, such as an interview or a pitch, give them a hook: I liked the guy with the spotty tie/I liked the lady in the purple jacket.

2 of Clubs – social media

The idea

It was alarming in being appointed to my most recent post to learn how much pre-research on me had already been undertaken online. As well as my CV and covering letter, the search firm and the nominations committee had access to my full and current profiles on Twitter, Facebook and LinkedIn. They could read all the blogs written by me since 2007 across a range of platforms, and watch me deliver a variety of talks and lectures on YouTube. They could read reviews of my books – and even my books if they had wanted to – all courtesy of a quick google. The Hinge Research Institute found that one in every three people turns to the internet immediately to look up someone they have heard about or are considering for an opportunity. So you have already well and truly lost control of your personal brand. You may or may not have been wise in your past, but you can make sure that your current and future online persona more accurately represents the professional you now are. But it does take a bit of investment.

The exercise

First, you need to google (and Bing) yourself. Then you need to look at each entry, at least three pages deep, across all of the categories on offer (images, news, videos and so on). Do you like what you see? Does it project the image you would like future employers or clients to see? How might you improve it?

Natasha Courtenay-Smith, the personal branding specialist and author, suggests you aim to own the entire first page of search results, so that people looking you up get a quick and reliable snapshot without going any further. The kinds of things that should come up are:

- your work website
- your social media profiles
- any official profiles
- any books or publications, by you or about you
- any talks you have given
- your awards or professional accolades
- any recent activity that shows you in a good light.

Most of these are in your gift, because search engines like recency, so you can crowd out less compelling backstory by keeping your profiles and online activity up to date. You can also trump less glamorous association by a few focused authority plays, like a profile in a big-hitter news publication. And if old stories crop up from zombie websites, you may be able to get them taken down.

Natasha's top tips for improving your on-line presence are:

1   update your website or online company profile and share it through social media;
2   keep at least two social media profiles current and active and link all of your profiles together so they automatically update each other;
3   participate in industry events and contribute articles to industry websites;
4   get yourself 'featured' by other websites, even if it is just your school's alumni page;
5   search engine results are about recency, relevance and authority, so feed the internet these things and they will soon start showing up on your search results.

All of this takes time, time you may not have, so be crafty about it. Is there anything you do anyway, that you could double-count on the internet, like retweeting news stories as you flick through, or reposting points of view you have delivered to clients, or sharing photos from interesting presentations you are attending? I imagine you would not attend a job interview in a crumpled suit, so take at least as much time over your online appearance as you do your physical appearance. It may be the difference between your being invited to that interview or not.

Chapter 8

Spades

Putting in the spadework

Our Spades are those practical tools and techniques that you need to get things done through others. Some of them are about investing in future potential through the likes of networking; some of them are about freeing yourself up to lead through the likes of delegating; and some of them are about how to get the best out of those around you, both in terms of problem-solving and performance. Use the table below to self-score as you read through the section.

Table 7 Spades

Spades		RAG	Next chance to practise
A♠	Difficult Conversations		
K♠	Numbers		
Q♠	Creativity		
J♠	Conflict		
10♠	Remaining Competitive		
9♠	Delegation		
8♠	Communication		
7♠	Public Speaking		
6♠	Meetings		
5♠	Networking		
4♠	Working the Room		
3♠	Mystery Shopping		
2♠	MECE		

Ace of Spades – difficult conversations

The idea

We all know the conversations we ought to have but are avoiding. And we all know that avoiding difficult conversations just makes them a lot worse and sends out a very negative message to everyone else. So, how can we get the words out? This is one skill that is definitely about practice. If you have already had a wide range of challenging conversations, you will have a whole library of templates to draw upon, which will reduce your sense of panic when you are looking into the hostile eyes of your difficult person.

Difficult conversations usually fall into one of three categories: difficult messages about performance, saying no, or asking for something tricky.

We have already met the slowest zebra, the one that distracts management and drags down team performance over time. This type of conversation only becomes 'difficult' if you do not create a culture of robust discussion and feedback; investing time in creating that sort of culture will reduce the time you have to spend dealing with things you could have nipped in the bud far earlier on. Getting into good feedback habits is your insurance against future difficult conversations. Equally, going ahead and actually having them will give you the muscle memory to make future ones far easier, so it is worth starting with some small vexations to build your skill. 'Please let me finish' to the interrupter. 'Could we hear from the people who haven't spoken yet?' to the ranter. 'I wonder if we might agree a process for you to warn me when you are about to miss a deadline in future?' to the procrastinator. You will have your pet peeves – stop feeding them, deal with them now. But remember that idea about 'stuck patterns' and watch for the energy – if it is all on your side, something is wrong.

There are two things that will help you with this skill. One is about vicarious learning; the other about walking. We have already met the finding about raised heart rate in those observing difficult conversations, so you could offer to accompany a colleague if they are going to a tricky client meeting or a tough negotiation. Or you could coach colleagues as part of their own development into being more robust in meetings. Or volunteer to be in-house faculty on a training programme to learn by watching others being put through their paces. Walking is the other thing that will help you. Our brains work faster when we are mobile, as a throwback to our hunter-gatherer days, so you can boost your cognitive resources by conducting conversations on the hoof. And with conversations that are awkward or likely to provoke emotion, walking has the added advantage of making it hard for you to see the other person's face. This is why parents gladly volunteer to be the teenage taxi, as the dim lighting and the lack of eye contact facilitates the sort of conversation they can no longer have with their children face-to-face. When walking outdoors, the cognitive resources you both save not having to school your face can then be used in the conversation, and the additional oxygen from being in the fresh air also boosts your brain better than the re-breathed air in the office. Walks, if you plan them well, are also time limited and can end up in a convenient coffee shop to agree next steps, or can allow the person to escape for some processing time before they return to the office.

Of all the skills we have met, this is the one to nail. That is why it is an ace. It is the ultimate apprentice piece. If you can have any conversation you need, as soon as you need to and in the right way, most challenges you face will simply melt away.

The exercise
Next time you need to say no, here is a handy routine, courtesy of the Personal Impact expert Sarah Cartwright:

- Say the person's name
- Acknowledge their request
- 'I'm going to say no'
- Give only 1 reason
- Offer an alternative if possible.

A conversation running this script might go as follows: 'Chris, I know you want me to stay late to finish this report. I'm going to say no, because I have to get home to put the children to bed. I can however brief Sarah to finish it for you and I will check it first thing tomorrow before we send it out.'

This is a very good routine to practise on your children and the person who always asks you to volunteer for things. The big ask is similar:

• Say the person's name
• Acknowledge that yours may be a difficult request
• 'I want to ask you ...'
• Give only 1 reason
• Offer something in it for them.

An example might be: 'Jo, I'm going to ask you an enormous favour. I want to ask if you would let me lead the client pitch tomorrow morning. It would be a great opportunity for me to get feedback from you about my performance. I would happily rehearse with you beforehand if that would make you more comfortable?'

Like all routines, both of these will feel clunky until they become a habit, so it is worth starting to use the formula now, so that when it really counts the words trip off your tongue. When could you next try these out?

King of Spades – numbers

The idea
One of the quickest ways to add value in a strategic conversation is to understand, instinctively, how a business model works, which levers are being discussed, and what would make the biggest difference to the bottom line. However, I am simply the worst person to advise you about numbers. Or perhaps I am the very best. Because when I look at them they make my brain freeze. Ironically, Maths was my best subject at school and I got my top score on my MBA for Statistics. Probably because I had to try so hard. So now I know I can do them when I have to. And you do have to. It is about managing risk. If you cannot, you will always be dependent on your finance director and if you ever get the wrong one you are sunk.

The exercise
If you already have a facility with numbers, rejoice! Now go and mentor someone who does not. If numbers are not your thing, start learning

about them now. It cost me several bottles of wine, but I used to plague my accountancy friends to take me through annual reports. Auditors are looking for fraud, so they are brilliant at telling you how numbers lie. And those pesky ratios? Brilliant – learn the whole lot and the annoying vocabulary that goes along with them. Then you will always be able to compare apples with pears and ask awkward questions about performance. The numbers are just a language for telling a story. So get someone to tell you the story first, then link it back to the numbers and you will be able to see why they are there.

You could start by looking at your organization's annual reports. If there is anything in them you do not understand, ask someone in accounts to take you through them. Looking back over the last five years, can you spot patterns and trends that you recognize from working there? Can you do the same for movements in the share price if your company is listed? You could also download annual reports for your key competitors or suppliers, if they are in the public domain. Again, what do they tell you? Can you compare year-on-year performance and guess the story that lies behind the numbers?

Queen of Spades – creativity

The idea

One way of defining strategy is to describe it as your organization's ability to out-think the competition. That is why I have included this section on creativity, rather than saddling you with a dull rehash about strategy tools. I am very keen on the quality of your thinking. In the last decade, we have focused so hard on improving the leader's interpersonal skill that we have quite neglected to boost their intellectual firepower too. Creativity is one way to limber up a mind that has got stuck in a business-as-usual rut.

Too often, 'creatives' are seen as brightly dressed mavericks with extraordinary vision, and if organizations have them in-house, they are kept in a ball-pit well away from the core business. But the creativity expert Annette Moser-Wellman describes the visionary as just one facet of creativity. In her 'Five Faces of Genius' model, she calls this face the

Seer: literally, one who sees. Such a person conjures up newness in their mind's eye, like the property developer who 'sees' the potential in an old ruin. The writer J. K. Rowling also talks of 'seeing' Harry Potter in the carriage, one magic day as her train sped south. But Moser-Wellman identifies four other 'faces'. One is the Sage, a person who innovates by simplifying things, stripping them back to their essence. No-frills airlines have based their entire business model on this face.

A third face is the Observer, a person who innovates by noticing detail. When Richard Branson noticed that the worst part of a frequent flier's journey was the trip to the airport, he introduced a limobike service to speed passengers past traffic to the check-in desk on a chauffeured motorbike. Apple is also famous for attention to detail. When engaging the voice dictation feature on newer Mac laptops, Apple automatically slows the internal fan speed so it can better hear your voice. Smartphone convergence, contactless payment cards, and even loyalty-card keyrings use similar attention to detail to innovate.

A fourth face is that of the Alchemist, who creates gold for businesses by mixing together ideas from different places. Doctors from Great Ormond Street Hospital called on the Ferrari and McLaren F1 teams to learn from the tight organization of their pit crews. In analysing the handover from the operating theatre to Intensive Care, they managed to reduce errors by 40 per cent. Interface carpets' biomimicry innovations are a further example of this kind of thinking, where Interface used the patterns of the forest floor to design modular tiling that could be laid in any combination, drastically reducing laying times and cost.

Moser-Wellman's final face is that of the Fool. Innovation in this mode arises from the absurd, or by turning things upside down. Rumour has it that when the Metropolitan Police wanted to improve their arrest rates for robbery, one bright spark suggested that they just ask burglars to hand over stolen goods. After his colleagues had stopped laughing, they played around with the idea and launched Operation Bumblebee. This increased their arrest rate because they worked closely with the pawn shops where burglars literally do hand over their stolen goods. Similarly, in London, a number of local authorities have been working on library innovation. When I was little, libraries were imposing buildings, up flights of stairs and full of books and silence and signs that said 'NO FOOD OR DRINK'. They were open while I was at school, which meant getting there was a bit tricky, and you had to join each library separately if you wanted to use more than one in your area. If you turn all of these variables upside down, you get Tower Hamlets' Idea Store concept. Purpose-built, user-friendly buildings co-located with the shops, with extended opening hours to match. Book clubs with wine to encourage participation, and partnerships with on-site coffee shops to get people to stick around. Lots of talking, lots of computers as well as books, and an electronic library card that works borough-wide. In the London Borough of Newham, this approach increased library visits by 239 per cent.

Moser-Wellman died in 2013, so her book's valediction now has extra resonance. Her thesis is that creativity is our gift and vocation and that finding ways to release it makes us fulfilled and happy. She likens it to bringing your soul to work, because her sense is that creativity springs from a well of genius that is our ancient birthright. Anyone can tap into it if they can master their imagination. For managers, in a field where the mythology differentiates between 'creatives' and 'uncreative' staff who tend to be the ones that stick to the detail or ask difficult questions, the Five Faces model serves as a reminder. Everyone can be creative, and innovation can surface through any or all of these channels.

The exercise

Next time you want to think differently about a problem or a challenge, try cycling through these five faces in turn, to see what they tell you. In general, when we talk about creativity we often talk in visual terms, about seeing things differently, looking through different eyes or different lenses. So the shortcut to creativity when you are stuck about something is to do anything that makes it look different, by changing it or changing you. An old proofreading trick is to change the font so that the writing looks unfamiliar and you have to read it more closely. Leaving your desk for a spell, or asking a colleague for advice, is also about shifting perspective. So is using a tool like the five faces, or drawing the problem, or reframing. So if you cannot see the solution, change how you see it. Hover above it and play with your parameters until an answer suggests itself.

Jack of Spades – conflict

The idea

We are brought up to believe that conflict is a negative thing, but actually conflict is revealing, and can be a useful way to generate innovation and better solutions to problems. One of these ways is what Silicon Valley used to call 'conflict capital' or the ability of an organization to sustain just the right amount of difference to let new thinking emerge, which in turn can be used by analysts as a barometer for assessing the innovation pipeline. While research on the superior performance of diverse teams is legion, some organizations still struggle to achieve this tricky Goldilocks mix, and some find that difference too easily becomes difficulty.

The classic model on interpersonal conflict is the Thomas-Kilmann model. It was devised by Kenneth Thomas and Ralph Kilmann in the 1970s, but remains surprisingly profound, and has been borne out by more recent mainstreaming of game theory. Broadly, they contrast two behaviours: assertion and co-operation. Different combinations and levels of these produce their five conflict-handling modes. If you do neither, you Avoid. If you mainly co-operate, you Accommodate. If you do a bit of both, you Compromise. If you mainly assert, you Compete. If you do lots of both, you Collaborate. Each has its place, and you need to be skilful at selecting and deploying the levers behind each mode to handle conflict well.

Of course, as my Cranfield colleague Veronica Burke often says, emotion is the confounding variable in all of this. It is hard to coolly select a mode when your hackles are up and you smell blood. Which is why this is a good one to practise when the conflict is something you notice but which does not directly affect you, for instance between colleagues or different departments. Honing your skills as a broker develops you vicariously, building your resourcefulness for when the conflict does affect you personally.

From time to time you will still experience what they call 'cognitive constriction', which is a tendency to see everything in black-and-white terms. This is a normal and well-meant neurobiological response to a threat. It is also why in 'flight' mode we develop tunnel vision. It is our reptilian brain trying to focus cognitive resource so we can survive the encounter. But most day-to-day conflicts are not life-threatening, even if our bodies are conditioned to respond as if they were. And cognitive constriction is the antithesis of good leading. It is also linked with highly negative depressive and suicidal states and feelings of panic and powerlessness. The conflict expert Sara Savage follows Thomas-Kilmann-style thinking in looking at conflict between religious views, advocating what she calls 'integrative complexity' as the best response. This is roughly the same concept as Theo Dawson's notion of Vertical Development, which we met in the context of the need for leaders to be able to handle an ever wider range of perspectives and ambiguity, while continuing to make wise decisions. So the more you flex that 'negative capability' muscle – your capacity to believe several impossible things before breakfast – the more you will also be able to cope with conflict. Your ability to suspend judgement, particularly under pressure, is a crucial meta-competence for leading.

The exercise

Next time you sense a looming disagreement, practise first your skills in assessment. Is this a battle worth fighting? What is at stake? Which values are in contrast, and is there a deeper common value that might suggest a resolution? This notion of 'super-ordinate goals' is why the Thomas-Kilmann model is so useful. Their 'Collaborate' mode is essentially about super-ordinate goals, the establishing of common ground and 'win-win' solutions. We know from Game Theory and Nash Equilibria, as explained in the movie *A Beautiful Mind*, that trying to establish a solution-set where both parties win is the best way to optimize outcomes. Mathematically speaking, it increases the size of the pie rather than focusing the conversation on how best to carve it up.

When you are in the midst of a disagreement, see if you can step outside of it to try to mediate, rather than getting sucked in on one side or the other. Get curious about the disagreement. What is each side trying to protect? What for them is being attacked by the difference of opinion? Often a dearly held value is being compromised, and a conflict response is generated as an attempt to restore it. Can you see a way through that might allow each party to be true to their values and beliefs, yet still agree on a joint course of action? Can you ask each side to talk a little about why they feel upset and to keep talking until some common ground becomes clear? Of course, not everything is susceptible to solution. Your contribution may not be to solve it, but to help the parties decide how best they can live with the co-existence of two competing 'truths' and to agree protocols for dealing with future differences of opinion.

10 of Spades – remaining competitive

The idea

The dilemma for any leader who wants to develop their mastery is whether their effort should focus on correcting their weaknesses or bolstering their strengths. The problem with the former is that addressing flaws just averages you out. And your flaws may or may not be career-limiting: they may be a sign you are in the wrong job with the wrong company. If feedback shows you are being held back by something, by all means address it. But otherwise, focus on your strengths. The logic for this comes from the economic idea of comparative advantage.

The Economist David Ricardo's 1817 explanation of comparative advantage used examples of wine and cloth in England and Portugal, but the notion can be put more simply. Apparently, Winston Churchill was a gifted bricklayer. But he was also a gifted politician and author. When he needed a wall built, he chose to pay builders to do his bricklaying for him, even though he could have done the work better himself. It made sense for him to do this, so he could spend his time on the activity – politics – where he had comparative advantage. To have done his own bricklaying would have taken him away from statecraft, so the opportunity cost of bricklaying made it unattractive for him.

Catholic Social Teaching has a similar concept, called subsidiarity, which is about seeing that things are carried out at the correct level. As enshrined in Article 5 of the Treaty on the European Union, subsidiarity means that decisions should be taken as closely as possible to the citizen. This idea about finding the right 'level' and playing to your comparative strengths is the best way to position yourself as an effective leader.

In my very first job, my boss had a word with me about doing the filing, which I had decided was one of my Friday afternoon activities. Of course, I was rather good at it, but he pointed out that my doing it took the work away from the filing clerk, and took me away from higher value-add activities which were more appropriate to my pay grade. As a leader you could probably also draft everyone's emails for them, and run every meeting, and make every decision, and attend every customer event. But it makes no sense for you to do so. It is wasteful of you as a resource and a waste of your talents as a leader. It is also a waste of the talents of those around you, who also want to do a good day's work.

For you to remain competitive as a leader, you must remain comparative. This is about how you choose to spend your time, and about matching your efforts to the appropriate level. Here is an example. As the leader, you have the absolute advantage – like Tiger Woods at golf or Michael Jordan at basketball – of being the leader. As Chairman of Gordonstoun, there are some activities it is best I do, not because I am the most skilled at them, but because they should be done by the Chairman. There might be things I am very good at like teaching leadership, but that activity is properly carried out by the teaching staff and not by school governors. So it would be indulgent of me to elbow teachers out of the way just because I quite like strutting my stuff. But equally there are things I might not gravitate towards, like interrogating the accounts, which nevertheless I must do, in my role as Chairman. Terry Leahy as CEO at Tesco used to stack the odd shelf while he was visiting stores, not because he thought the staff could not manage, but as a way of demonstrating solidarity and reinforcing his personal brand.

In formal strategy terms, Gary Hamel explains that a 'me too' strategy based on absolute competition inevitably leads to 'corporate liposuction' as competitors match each other's incremental changes in a race to the bottom. Price wars among the supermarkets are a case in point. Those who compete 'enough' but keep a focus on their comparative advantage will tend to emerge as stronger brands over the long term, like the Waitrose and Marks and Spencer food offers in the UK. Their competitors, differentiating on price, become commodities in comparison. And a commodity strategy attracts little customer loyalty, especially with the dawn of internet shopping. So both personally and organizationally, be careful who you choose to be your pace-setter. By all means benchmark your skills, but set your own criteria of excellence and plan to exceed them on an on-going basis. Your strengths are what will differentiate you, not a lack of weaknesses.

The exercise

Draw two overlapping circles. One is about your role: what does the person occupying this role need to do? The other is about your inhabitation of it: what particular stamp can you put on this role, given your strengths and weaknesses? It is likely there will be a pretty close match, but pay attention to the margins. Is there anything you need to choose to do, because it would otherwise not come naturally to you? And, is there anything you need to choose not to do, because it is no longer appropriate?

Once you have applied this thinking to yourself, you might like to apply it to your organization. Comparative advantage is an invitation to focus your effort where you can best generate a tradable excess – it is about locating your value-add. In some sense, comparative advantage is about generating intrinsic competition, to hone whatever talent it is that you have, like 'adaptation' in evolutionary biology. This is different from the usual way in which we look at competing externally, because the development agenda is set by the talent. A compulsion to outpace competitors locks you into an agenda set by them, and competition becomes just about copying. If they downsize, outsource or cut prices, the logic of competitive advantage suggests that you should do likewise. The logic of comparative advantage argues instead that you should focus on the area of activity where you are at your best.

9 of Spades – delegation

The idea

Apart from the Dilbert cartoons, it was David Bolchover who first broke ranks to argue in 2005 that the issue was not stress and overwork at work, it was how dull most work is. While 'senior management' are galloping from vital meeting to vital meeting, many of the people around them are going quietly batty with boredom. Since then, the statistics on staff engagement and absenteeism have got worse. Gallup's current disengagement figure is 87 per cent of employees worldwide, which is a devastating indictment of leaders everywhere. And if you have read as many staff surveys as I have, you will notice a trend across industries that junior staff feel senior staff do not trust them enough and do not give them interesting work to do. Please, if your staff are that rubbish, sack them. If they are not, stop hogging work and pass it down.

If you cannot delegate, the fault is either yours or theirs. If it is theirs, you need to have those difficult conversations about why they cannot take on tasks, or get them the training and support to be able to do so. But having wrestled with many a leader on this topic over the years, usually the delegation does not happen because the leader does not want it to enough. If they are in a rush to go on holiday, or something urgent comes up, they happily off-load even the knottiest of tasks, but when business as usual returns somehow they are overloaded again. Just imagine what you could do to add value to your organization if you had more time. You would do, if you were better at delegating.

The exercise

The first step in delegating is not to grab the nearest matrix and apply it to your in-tray, it is to take a good long hard look in the mirror. If you were to adopt the 'lead through, learn from' rule of thumb, what is stopping you delegating everything in your diary? What would you need to do to ensure that you could, at least theoretically? If you cannot, you are an organizational risk, because if anything happens to you, business as usual is in jeopardy.

I imagine your workload splits roughly as follows. Stuff you have to do because someone has asked you to. Stuff you said you would do and now you are stuck with it. Stuff you quite like doing. Stuff it is quicker for you to do than to delegate. Stuff you have put off doing, so it would be too embarrassing to ask anyone else to take it on now. And probably some other stuff. Imagine we took your ego out of the equation. If you did not care how it looked, would that help? Now look through your list again. If you had to delegate every single thing on it, write down how you would go about it. Then set yourself a target to move further towards that goal. Is there one particularly weak team member who is making you loath to delegate, and how could you address their capability? Are you too busy to delegate, and can you block out some time to make progress on that front? Could you clear your plans to delegate with whoever you are trying to impress, so that they are instead awestruck by your leadership and commitment to staff development?

8 of Spades – communication

The idea
If you ever review a group task, or survey employees, the one finding you can guarantee is that people think there should be better communication. It is not exactly clear what this means, and it may be a euphemism, but it is nevertheless true that communication is the signal task of the leader. So, here is a handy communications audit tool from my Deloitte days. I came up with it on the back of some beermats, nursing a drink with my colleague Jane Falconer-White in the old temperance hall in Putney. You can use it to structure your communications, or to audit them when something has gone wrong. ANIMATES – ANnouncement, Imperative, Media, Audience, Timing, Environment and Sender (see Table 8).

The exercise
What have you currently got on your to-do list that presents you with the opportunity to deploy brilliance in your communication? I used this tool to review project and team communications, and to plan

reports and messages. You can use it to plan or to review any communication, and it is a good mental checklist before you press send on an important message. Work through each of the elements in turn, to check you have thought of everything. What does it tell you about your defaults or your blind spots for next time?

Table 8 ANIMATES

ANnouncement What are you trying to say? Is it in the right language? Does it make sense and is it compelling?

Imperative Why are you sending this message and why do they need to read it? If you do not make this clear, or there is no good reason, do not expect them to make time for it. What is in it for them?

Media What is your channel strategy? It is likely that you will need to vary your channel by audience. Some may not have access to email, or find accessing voicemail abroad a chore. Is the version of software you are using the same as the one your recipients use?

Audience Can you segment your audience, both in terms of how best to communicate with them and how you might prioritize them? It may be that there are some audiences who would be happy with a generic email, while others would need a personal meeting.

Timing When is the best time to send this message out? How frequently might you need to repeat it, and do you need to vary this by audience? Time zones, peak times on Twitter, etc?

Environment What are the local variations in culture, style or practice that you need to take into account? One of my high-tech clients discovered that an unusually high number of staff were checking the corporate homepage every day. Not because they were good citizens, but because they all had stock options and the homepage had a stock price ticker on it. So, positioning updates right next to this ticker meant they could reach more staff than just sending them an email.

Sender Whose emails do they always read? Who needs to deliver this message for it to be heard? Do you need to vary the messenger by audience, or reinforce it through a range of trusted messengers? Tea lady, driver, grapevine and gossip.

7 of Spades – public speaking

The idea

The actor Laurence Olivier famously suffered from stage fright, and was sick in a bucket before going on to perform. A story (probably apocryphal) holds that, when asked how he coped, he said: 'I send on Mr Technique and hope to follow him later.' I do not think anyone loves public speaking or does not get nervous about it – they just get used to it if they do it a lot. In my time at Ashridge, I taught for at least 4,000 hours. So if it takes 10,000 hours to achieve mastery, it should not be surprising if I look unfazed by giving a talk, because I am almost half-way there. And I know that if my heart rate is raised by nerves, I am likely to be better on my feet, because my brain will work faster, so it is important that I do not over-prepare. If I do, I am inclined to forget my lines, because my brain is not optimized for the task.

When I did my MBA, Sir David Tweedie was Chairman of the Accounting Standards Board. He came in to talk to the students. We, of course, were dreading it. A whole hour on accounting standards. Then in walks this quiet man, full of jokes about how boring he is. Of course, we were transfixed and he made the time fly past. He also taught me a valuable lesson about confidence. You will not get found out if you find yourself out first. One person I taught in the Foreign Office had a dreadful stutter. He was so worried that it would emerge during meetings that he rarely said a word. We devised a routine whereby he would read out a script at the start of the meeting, where he would tell people that he had a stutter and say that it got worse whenever he felt strongly about something. So, if he did dry up, could they just wait, because it was a sign that he had something rather important to say. This took the tension out of the situation, so that he was rarely thereafter affected; but if he was, they would wait until he was ready to go on. It takes enormous courage to make yourself vulnerable, but if you risk it, the humanity in those around you will tend to respond.

The exercise

Thinking about your next opportunity for public speaking, how will you structure it? You can spend a lot of time and money answering this question. Rules of three, visuals, strong openings and closings – you know all this because you sit through a lot of speeches. But it is quite another thing when you have to deliver them yourself. So by all means structure the thing into next week. You can always fall back on the famous dictum attributed to Aristotle: 'tell them what you are going to tell them; tell them; then tell them what you just told them.' Most importantly, though, prepare yourself well. Think about how you want them to be left feeling – that is what will ultimately remain. And practise, a lot. Use your phone to video yourself or get a friend to do so, so that you are familiar with your instrument. And ask for feedback after every speech, so that you build up a picture of your range and vulnerabilities.

You are probably better than you think you are, too. There are a couple of times recently when I have felt I was dying on stage, but when I watch the video back I look as cool as a cucumber. And, if you want the shortcut, get yourself some press training. Learning to deliver both radio and TV interviews under fire is by far the best way to learn resilience. Because the thing we most fear is heckling or hostile Q&A. You can tell who the novices are, because when they get a stinker from the audience they actually step back, as though struck. So always step into a question. If it is particularly awful, reflect it back to the questioner to check you have heard it correctly, which gives you thinking time. You might ask others to offer their thoughts before you reply. Then you can decide whether you tackle it head-on, take it offline, or do the politician's thing of 'what a great question, which reminds me ...'. An even better version of this evasion is to use 'bridging'. Many interviewers are so used to being fobbed off that they will just keep digging if you avoid the question. But if you address the question but quickly move on to something you would rather say, it makes it hard for them to re-ask the original question without appearing rude. So, you could, for instance, say something like: 'you've asked about my research base for that statistic. It's from an article I read recently, when I also read an extremely good argument for the pivotal contribution of employee engagement – I can send you that if you like.'

Use props, use stories, avoid notes. Particularly avoid using PowerPoints as your notes, because you will bore both yourself and your audience. If you do need notes, practise with them so there is no fumbling or distraction, and explain them away: 'I have some notes here so that

I don't get too carried away ...', or similar. And use eye contact, with both wings of the room (you will probably have a bias and a corresponding blind spot). Avoid addressing yourself exclusively to the most important person in the room, because everyone can see you doing it and they feel disrespected.

6 of Spades – meetings

The idea

Virgin's Richard Branson likes to hold his meetings standing up, or walking. Google's Larry Page changed the default from hour-long meetings to fifty minutes, to allow for breaks and to keep everyone on time. Tesco incorporates a brief 'benefits and concerns' review at the end of each of theirs. There are as many books on effective meetings as there are on leadership, but I assume you have sat through enough by now to have figured out what makes a good one or not. But have you yet figured out how to use them to their fullest advantage?

Looking at your diary for a typical week, how long do you spend in meetings? My guess is that it is at least 20 per cent of your time. This tends to increase the more senior you get. Imagine that these meetings were front-loaded end-to-end in your diary. If you started them on New Year's Day, you would be into March before you were done. And whenever they are polled, workers report that most meetings seem to be a waste of time. I want to suggest a better way to think about this use of your time. It is actually free training.

The exercise

Next time you sigh when you spy a meeting in your calendar, decide to rejoice instead and schedule it in as a learning opportunity. For the apprentice, meetings are pivotal. They are where you learn about colleagues and culture and the business you are in, and they are your opportunity to try things out. You could practise your listening skills, you could practise excellent questions, you could identify the different styles on display and assess them in your day book. You could practise summarizing, or rationing your contributions, or eliciting the thoughts of the quieter contributors. You could improve your personal impact by planning your appearance, contributions and style beforehand. If the opportunity can be created, you could practise your presentation skills, or apply some creativity or problem-solving tools; and events during the meeting provide the data for you to seek or offer colleagues feedback afterwards.

5 of Spades – networking

The idea

I have a hunch that if we were to repeat our research in ten years' time, networking would feature more prominently. Increasingly, it is where you find your next job and it is where you find help when you need it the most. But does anyone really enjoy 'networking?' I think most people enjoy meeting interesting people, and most people enjoy being able to make connections between people they know. But the last thing most of us want to do at the end of a busy week is to sip warm white wine while listening to a dull speaker in an anonymous hotel, just to swap business cards with some faceless individuals. At least when we did that in the playground the cards had nice pictures on them.

A good network is a live version of Google. No matter what you face or who you need to reach, you will be able to, if you have a strong and current network. We have a lot of social media tools to facilitate this these days, but they need to be fed through occasional live meetings. The social-networking guru Euan Semple makes it a practice to phone up contacts he has not seen in a while, to renew the contact before it lapses.

The exercise

Here are my rules:

1 Next time you are invited to something, if you are free and there might be people there you should meet, go, even if it is just for one drink.
2 When you meet someone at an event, do not look over their shoulder – give them your full attention.
3 If someone you trust suggests you meet so-and-so, do so. Even if you do not know why. It will be worth it.

4   Never keep score – do favours willy-nilly; it will either reward you, or build your character.
5   Always help out headhunters.
6   Volunteer and take on roles outside of your main job.
7   Always carry business cards with you, even to the gym and on holiday.

4 of Spades – working the room

The idea

Maybe we have gone overboard with 'stranger danger', but we seem to be losing our ability to strike up conversations with people we do not know. And it is most people's worst nightmare to have to enter a room full of strangers and emerge triumphant. But there are many people for whom this is the bread-and-butter of their job and they have a lot to teach us. First, dress code. Always check, or google images from last year's event to gauge the form. You will be at an instant disadvantage if you are wrongly attired. I once swanned into a Foreign Office party, in full regalia and in full-length velvet, only to realize that the invitation had said dinner suit not dinner jacket. All the other ladies were in fresh summer dresses, so I had to work my way around the perimeter, stowing jewellery and gloves in various flower pots until my status matched theirs. That said, if you need to stand out, you might want to match the status of the highest-status people present, or dress more formally than you usually do. Just do so deliberately and with caution, so that you do not look foolish.

If you are attending a large reception where you do not know anyone, start with a Mission. The default mission is always to find a drink. This allows you to scan the room for 'people like me'. They might be on their own, look the same age, or be dressed similarly; or they might be people you recognize. When you have found a person or group that looks appropriate, introduce yourself into the discussion. This can feel daunting if they are already in a tight-knit circle, but you can normally get 'in' by using direct eye contact with the ring-leader or whoever is holding court, or you can lurk. Lurking works well because no one likes having their personal space invaded. If you are too close, they will automatically step back to let you into the circle. Or you can pick off stragglers with small talk, or you can tow a waiter over to refresh drinks, inveigling your way in while he sows confusion. If you cannot get in, stride off confidently and regroup in the cloakroom.

Next, small talk. Luckily the British have evolved a highly sophisticated routine for connecting with strangers: talking about the weather. Visitors to Britain are left puzzled by this national obsession, but, as the anthropologist Kate Fox points out, talking about the weather is nothing to do with the weather. She likens it to primate grooming and social bonding and says that initiating an exchange about the weather is British code for 'I'd like to talk to you – will you talk to me?' Perhaps the America of Louis Armstrong is not so different: 'I see friends shaking hands, saying how do you do, they're really saying I love you.' Handshakes in any case date back to the days when there was a need to show your sword arm was not engaged, so perhaps it really is as simple as letting the other person know that you wish them well, however you choose to convey this message.

After you have exhausted the weather, a topic may naturally follow. At this stage, Jane Austen would recommend moving on to discuss the roads. Opine on religion, politics or sex at your peril, but if you get brain freeze, just think golf and all those chaps in plus-fours shouting 'FORE' when they tee off:

- Family – questions about children, or where people come from
- Occupation – questions about job, location and career
- Recreation – questions about hobbies, holidays and enthusiasms
- Education – questions about schooling (of them or aforementioned children)

In Edinburgh, the first question you are traditionally asked is where you went to school. Maybe that is just an Edinburgh thing. Nevertheless, I include the category because it remains the prevailing preoccupation of so many parents. If you have tried all of this and have still not got any traction, an ambassador once leaked to me his wife's emergency question, which seems to work globally. Sidle up to them furtively and ask: 'how is the situation in the North?'

Now, what to do if you find the one conspiracy theorist in the room? If you get stuck, make an excuse about seeing someone you know or finding a waiter, and move on: 'I really mustn't monopolize you ...'. If you are accompanied, you can agree a deal with your companion for mutual rescue if either of you gets stuck. Private Secretaries are brilliant at 'urgent phone calls' from major heads of state and you may be able to arrange something similar. One veteran Head of Mission used to have to visit several embassies of an evening, which he would do at great speed, having secured a back exit for each one and a route through that would make him highly visible to the key stakeholders there.

If you are glad-handing, make handshakes firm, brief, and accompanied by good eye contact. Do not panic about remembering names. Either you will make a connection and end up with a business card, or you will be able to look back at photos or a guest list. If you have to introduce someone to a person whose name you do not know, bluff your way through with hyperbole, or by suggesting common ground. 'Do meet this interesting person, who like you adores Tintoretto.' You can always fetch a waiter to cover over your gaffe, or just beam through it, looking comfortable, until the moment has passed.

The exercise

Look at your diary and identify an event you are planning to attend that feels intimidating. Or if you have turned down an invitation because you cannot face working the room, say 'yes' to the next one. Beforehand, sit down with this section and work through it. Check the dress code, consult the guest list, plan your arrival and exit, and read this again on your way there. When you arrive, deploy this routine and see what you learn from it. Go armed with FORE and some business cards and keep smiling. Resist the temptation to stand in the corner glued to your phone looking busy. Good luck.

3 of Spades – mystery shopping

The idea

There is a famous story about how ad agency Allen Brady & Marsh won the British Rail account. When the client turned up for the pitch, an uninterested receptionist, filing her nails, made them wait in the foyer, which was crowded with coffee-stained tables and overflowing ashtrays. The minutes ticked by. Nobody came to meet them. Furious, the BR team was about to storm out when Marsh and his team appeared. 'That's how the public sees BR,' Marsh told them. 'Now let's see what we can do to put it right.'

Mystery shopping is primarily about overcoming blind spots. Not only might you as a leader have become remote from the sharp end of your business, you may also have staff who feed you what they think you want to hear instead of telling you what is actually going on.

The exercise
A useful discipline is to keep a close eye on role model organizations in your sector. Can you map them, and find a way to become a customer, a client, a supplier or a neighbour? Or can you use your networks to get unvarnished feedback from those who are?

You might also like to do some mystery shopping in your own business, if there is a safe way to do it. The Post Office Counters' senior management always had a 'back to the floor' discipline and every year they would spend a few days serving behind the counter to remind themselves what it was like. Perhaps this is something you could do, too, or ask a friend to become a customer of yours and solicit their feedback?

2 of Spades – MECE

The idea
It has become so important these days to correct the cognitive bias in both managerial education and style in order to promote emotional competence that we have quite neglected thinking. In particular, how to think well. This exercise will give you brain-ache, because I am going to encourage you to unpack your brain, set it going in slow motion, and try to spot what it is up to. So if you are not in that kind of mood, by all means return to this section later.

Those McKinsey types are very good at thinking, because they do it for a living. Scour any bookcase in their offices and you will find their bible. It is written by Barbara Minto, who writes about logic trees and is very keen on structured thinking. We know from psychological profiling and recruitment that many senior leaders are the type of strategic thinker inclined to intuit a vision or direction, then feel the need to prove themselves right through its success. This can often work, but is risky, as steps in the logic may have been missed. What thinking processes like Minto's do is slow down a busy brain and check that fruitful 'routes to solution' have not been overlooked, or filtered out by pre-emptive judgement about what would usually work or find favour.

It works like this. What is your issue? I want to know what to have for breakfast. Well, to answer that question we need to split the dilemma into 'Mutually Exclusive, Collectively Exhaustive' (MECE) categories. You could have a cooked or an uncooked breakfast. Cooked is not uncooked and uncooked is not cooked (mutually exclusive). Together they constitute the sum total of breakfast options (collectively exhaustive), if you are to eat at all. Each branch of this tree gives you further options, for example dairy and non-dairy. Following the cooked/dairy route suggests eggs, following the uncooked/dairy suggests yoghurt. And so on. You might find the logic suggesting that you eat uncooked bacon, and while you are busy worrying about food poisoning you realize that charcuterie for breakfast might be exactly what you fancy.

Here is a business example, courtesy of the MECE guru Paul Davies. Your numbers are flat. You need to boost profits. How? Well, you need to do that both in the short term and in the long term, and by increasing revenues or cutting costs. Both of these categories are Mutually Exclusive and Collectively Exhaustive. The costs, when you look at them, will be fixed or variable. Fixed and variable as categories are mutually exclusive; fixed + variable is collectively exhaustive ...

The kind of graphic this produces (see Figure 6) looks fiendishly complex. Indeed, clients pay a lot of money for this kind of thing. But it is, simply, logic. Can you steel yourself to pore over it? If you can get your head around it, you will save your organization a fortune in consultancy fees. It is a useful discipline in and of itself. But MECE is also useful as a concept, because it allows you to listen to problems and

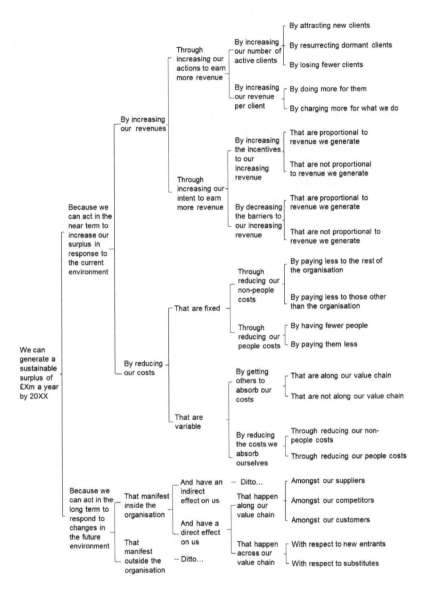

Figure 6 MECE tree

ask better questions about them. Quite often you will be presented with a solution, but it may not solve the right problem. This kind of logic will help you unpick whether or not it is the right one, and whether any other solutions have been prematurely rejected or overlooked.

The exercise

Next time you are making a decision, before you settle on something, audit your thinking to slow it down. Aim for dichotomies. Try to construct your own MECE logic tree. Do not edit out stuff that 'won't fly,' because it might, if you look at it differently. And boiling it back down to its essentials might reveal that an option you have written off, with a little work, might just solve your problem.

Chapter 9

Hearts

Putting others at ease

Do you remember all those pictures of dated ladies parading up and down with books on their heads, or curtsying to cakes? One of the institutions that used to churn out these ladies in droves, generally to go husband-shopping during the Season, was the famous Lucie Clayton College in Gloucester Road, Kensington. Joanna Lumley went there, as did Jean Shrimpton and Tara Palmer-Tomkinson. I went there, too. They still had the famous model car – just the passenger seat, because 'ladies don't drive' – and they taught us how to get in and out of it without showing our knickers. I also know how to walk with a book on my head, how to glide down a staircase, and how to pose for a 'girls in pearls' photo. It was all quite a hoot and I have dined out on it ever since. But behind the jokes I learned something serious and very useful. Amid all the tips on etiquette, man handling and appearance, was the insight that manners are simply about putting others at their ease. Being well-mannered is quite the most generous and socially useful thing you can ever do.

My mother tells the story of some Polish soldiers, far away from home, still stationed in Scotland after the war had ended. Her mother had invited them round for tea. Granny's teas were legendary. A crisp tablecloth over a table groaning with sandwiches, scones, cakes, and a bewildering array of homemade jams. Granny passed one of the soldiers a pot of jam. It had a spoon in it. He looked rather bewildered, then took up the spoon and started to eat the jam. My mother felt a sharp elbow dig into her ribs, as Granny passed her a pot of jam and gestured that she should follow suit. This she did, and it smoothed over a social awkwardness which would have been the opposite of the hospitality intended towards some loyal, brave and lonely soldiers.

These finishing schools were not called 'Charm Schools' for nothing. The famous British Public School – and the likes of Sandhurst,

Dartmouth or Cranwell for the military – did the same for men. Looking at these institutions with today's eyes, we tend to be critical. But one thing they did was to prepare people well for social occasions. And what is work if not just an elaborate and on-going social occasion? When the leadership books talk about 'charisma' this is part of what they mean: the ability to be charming and to endear yourself to those around you. Not all leadersmithing will involve being nice, but it will tend to get you rather further in life than being right. So my Hearts are all about charm, and your ability to make those around you feel at ease in your company: confident and able to be themselves. Because this is truly where they need to be to be able to perform well for you. Old-fashioned ideas about carrot and stick simply do not work as well as the unleashing of loyalty, creativity and discretionary effort from people who actually like you. Use the table below to self-score as you read through the section.

Table 9 Hearts

Hearts		RAG	Next chance to practise
A♥	Manners		
K♥	Trust		
Q♥	Listening		
J♥	Questions		
10♥	Eye Contact		
9♥	Storytelling		
8♥	Relationships		
7♥	Choreographed Conversations		
6♥	Coaching		
5♥	Teams		
4♥	Feedback		
3♥	Thank Yous		
2♥	Character		

Ace of Hearts – manners

The idea

'Manners Makyth Man' is famously the motto of William of Wykeham and the foundations he established, New College in Oxford and Winchester College in Hampshire. A bit old school, you might think and a bit 1370s. Yet the new Marylebone Boys School, a free school that opened in 2014, chose to focus its aims not only on academic rigour, but also on 'good behaviour'.

In the context of nurturing creative conflict, friction may be necessary for traction. But day-to-day interactions between people generally go better if they are greased with charm. I think this is to do with your 'use cost'. Have you ever lost out to someone who is probably nowhere near as good as you, but they are more 'popular'? Have you ever had feedback that the other person was a better 'cultural fit' than you? When we are talking about colleagues, we often use euphemisms like 'poor people skills' or 'limited Emotional Intelligence', but basically it means that they are hard work, so their use cost is higher than the alternative. You know who these people are, because whenever they show up you have a voice in your head coaching you through the conversation. This is your executive function actively managing your response to them so that you are not rude, which is why it drains your energy.

You might remember the scene in the movie *When Harry Met Sally*, when Harry explains to Sally that she is 'high maintenance' because she is so particular about everything. Probably like Sally, we are all great and well worth the investment. But you will know yourself that if you have a choice of two colleagues, you will choose the one who is easier to do business with. Most of the leaders I know have a chronic problem with energy, and need to husband it carefully. We know leaders sleep badly and have cognitive overload, so they are not blessed with a lot of bandwidth for effortful people. And being patient with high-maintenance people saps energy. It is the thing that leaders consistently name as their worst mood sucker. So if a colleague is rather wearing and the leader is already exhausted, why would they bother? In physics, inertia is about conserving energy, so any premium demanded needs to be well worth it.

The exercise

The best way to reduce your use cost is to raise your level of charm. The author and bon viveur Bill Coles learned charm the hard way, as a reporter for *The Sun* newspaper, trying to get stories from reluctant interviewees. In his book, *Red Top*, he argues that you just have to schedule in the practice, so that when you need to be brilliant at it you already are. Do it every morning, at the paper shop. At the bus stop. Buying coffee. Buying lunch. Phoning a call centre. Chatting at the school gates. Any interaction can be practice, if you give the person your full attention. His golden rules are about showing an interest in the other person's life, displaying impeccable manners, and saying 'thank you' afterwards. So you might chat to your cabbie about the roadworks, the receptionist about how busy she seems, and the cashier about the bag charge. Anything that allows you to show charm. Lest you feel this is slightly cynical, do remember how good you feel when even the most ordinary interaction turns out to be a pleasure. We should be doing this all the time anyway.

King of Hearts – trust

The idea

In 2012, some researchers decided to find out what made people trust health professionals. Moyez Jiwa and a team from Curtin University in Australia visited community pharmacies and showed customers a series of random photographs of men wearing varying combinations of medical equipment: stethoscope, reflex hammer, surgical scrubs, otoscope and pen. People were then asked to rate the man as honest, trustworthy, honourable, moral, ethical, genuine – or a combination thereof. The results showed that we are much more likely to trust a 'doctor' if they are wearing three or more items of medical equipment and especially a stethoscope. Trust is particularly salient in any professional setting, because instant rapport saves valuable time and money. Particularly in the medical and legal professions, you are not likely to get the facts out of vulnerable people if they do not trust you.

Trust is a nebulous concept. How can we define it in a way that allows us to understand it better, particularly if, as a leader, our job is to attract it? What is our equivalent of a stethoscope and white coat? Thanks to David Maister, Charles Green and Robert Galford, we have an answer. Their 'Trust Equation' holds that trust is a function of someone's Credibility, Reliability and Intimacy.

Credibility is the degree to which you know what you are talking about. Do you have the relevant qualifications or experience? Do you sound compelling and certain? Do you look the part? Hence the stethoscope!

Next, **Reliability**. Are you constant? Do you always deliver on your promises, even down to the detail of your time-keeping, by meeting deadlines and by following up well? Or does your performance vary with mood and circumstance?

Lastly, **Intimacy**. Even if your CV is loaded with evidence of your credibility and reliability, people always want face-to-face interviews, because we trust people, not documents. What hooks are you giving out to allow the other person to connect with you? This might be about common ground, but it could as easily be an exchange about the weather, if it allows you to relate as people.

No matter how much you do to build trust, it can still be torpedoed by what Maister and team call **Self-orientation**. This relates to the agenda – are you on their agenda or your own? If we ever feel as though the other person is playing us, we are suspicious of their motives and we stop trusting them. So how transparent are you being about your agenda with the other person, and how can you best balance this through Intimacy so that it does not affect your Credibility or Reliability?

The exercise

They say that trust arrives on foot, but leaves on horseback. Where in your professional life could you do with a trust boost? The thinking behind the Trust Equation can be used either to audit a relationship that has somehow gone wrong, or to plan a new interaction to try to establish instant rapport. It is a good way to structure your standard introduction, too. You might think it is disarming to be self-effacing, but it may prevent you from establishing your credibility with a key audience. It is also a useful way to see why trust fails at a macro level. Charities that take a cut from an energy deal that they sell to the vulnerable? Politicians who charge expenses for items that are nothing to do with public office? Bankers and business leaders who award themselves eye-watering bonuses even when profits plummet? These are all examples of Self-orientation scuppering trust. Also, Credibility can be lost if results have been faked or CVs contain lies; Reliability takes a knock when a bad year interrupts an unbroken record of continual profitability, or a leader makes an unguarded remark. And Intimacy is affected every time a leader or a business under the microscope says 'no comment' and retreats off-site for a behind-closed-doors pow-wow. So when you spot an opportunity to establish a relationship or shore up trust, use this approach to plan how you might best go about it.

Queen of Hearts – listening

The idea

You have been listening since you were in the womb, of course. Plenty of time to develop some bad habits. Like selective listening or editing or fast forward, because you already know what they are going to say. Zoning out or waiting to speak or interrupting? When I ask people to listen to each other in a structured way, it is quite terrifying how much data they are able to pick up. Perhaps we are lucky we are generally listened to so badly. And the response from the person being listened to well? They tend to feel somehow cleansed and honoured.

The exercise

One way to improve your staff engagement scores is to give your staff a really good listening to, because it makes them feel noticed. The exercise we use at Ashridge is about imagining three 'levels' of listening. Of course in practice these blur, but trying to separate out the channels raises your awareness about which you find easiest and which you perhaps routinely neglect. The levels are:

1 Facts – hoovering up the data and reflecting it back as accurately as you can, without notes.

2   Emotions – spotting tone, inflection, body language – anything that conveys the person's feelings about the topic, then playing this back as a hypothesis to test understanding.

3   Intuition – accessing your 'sixth sense' about what you are hearing – images, notions, metaphors, anything that might be data for them: 'I had an image in my mind of a tightrope walker – is that how you are feeling?'

You can try this in your next meeting or one-to-one, and channel-surfing between the levels will help you to stop your mind from wandering.

You may be one of those people whose brain just works terribly fast. You are listening, of course, but you respond so quickly that the listener supposes you were actually just waiting to speak. So, as well as actually listening, you need to appear to be listening to achieve the full effect.

Table 10 Listening

Simple echoing	Repeating back the last word or last few words, as a prompt for them to continue talking, to demonstrate attention, interest and as an invitation to continue
Selective echoing	Repeating back a salient or loaded word or phrase, in order to probe deeper or to invite them into new territory
Open questions	Participant-centred questions to elicit self-directed exploration and discovery
Closed questions	Questions to check understanding or to demonstrate empathy, e.g. 'that must have been hard?'
Empathetic divining	Naming something unsaid, e.g. 'it sounds as if you feel worried about that'
Checking for understanding	Clarifying for you both: 'let me see, are you saying that ...?' to invite correction or confirmation
Paraphrasing	Showing solidarity by reflecting back in your own words something important that they have said
Logical marshalling	Organizing and summarizing what you have heard to bank it and move on to the next topic

John Heron has a useful list of the kinds of approaches you might use to help you to demonstrate that you are listening well. Writing in 1989, before the current enthusiasm for 'being in the moment', he describes the approach as 'be here now, be there now, giving free attention'. He suggests that, once you are fully present, you deploy the eight gambits described in Table 10.

In choosing your questions, he cautions preferring 'following' questions to leading ones, to help you stay on the other person's agenda and not veer off onto your own. You may of course want to offer hypotheses to stimulate their thinking, but if the exercise is both about actual listening and about being seen to listen well, staying with their agenda for as long as possible is most likely to achieve these goals.

Jack of Hearts – questions

The idea

What is a question? In speaking, we use vocal inflection to indicate a question, and on paper we use a question mark like that one. In doing so, we are differentiating them from statements. A statement may or may not require a response. A question, unless it is rhetorical, always does. So a question also requires thought. It is my invitation to you to switch your brain on. This is why using questions can have the effect of making those around you think you are wise, because you provoke them to think.

You will be familiar with the various types of questions there are, but here is a recap for you.

Closed – a question that invites an answer of yes or no
Example: Did you kill Caesar?

Open – a question that invites a more expansive response
Example: Who did you see at the Theatre of Pompey that day?

Leading – a question intended to direct the answer
Example: You did, did you not, on the Ides of March, approach the Emperor with a dagger, intending to stab him?

Rhetorical – a question for effect that is not designed to be answered
Example: *Et tu, Brute?*

When my sister trained as an advocate she used to use me as target practice. And thinking of questions in courtroom categories can help you to select the right type. Are you in Direct Examination or Cross-Examination? The former is about trying to elicit testimony from a witness (simple 'single-fact' open questions that gently build a picture, step-by-step). The latter is about trying to expose flaws in a case to win your argument (leading questions that hammer home the point you are trying to make). Whether you are in direct examination or in cross-examination will inform the tack you take and the results you achieve. When you know which 'mode' you are in, you can choose which individual questions to ask. To help, you may recall Rudyard Kipling's famous poem from the *Just So Stories*, which starts:

I keep six honest serving-men
    (They taught me all I knew);
Their names are What and Why and When
    And How and Where and Who.

This is a good menu for questions, but remember that each will take you in a different direction. *Why* can feel accusatory or can send the person into an elaborate retrospective, which keeps them in the past rather than focusing on solutions for the future; equally it can usefully check assumptions and open up new trains of thought. *When* is rather a closed question, so will give you information but may not add much; equally it can be a useful way to raise awareness of the context in which the situation occurs. *How* can be a bit too global a question and inspire too intellectual a response; equally it might be the best way to broach options. *Where* and *Who* are usefully specific, especially if they are used at the right stage in the process, but tend again to lead to closed questions that elicit information. *What* is possibly the most useful, because it invites specificity, as long as the questions are for their benefit and not just to fill gaps in your own knowledge.

The exercise
Start your review of skill in the use of questions by indulging in a bit of meeting bingo on question categories: open, closed, leading, rhetorical.

Are you good at spotting the different types? How many were deployed in your meeting and to what effect? If you are feeling brave, you could ask a colleague to apply the list to you in your next meeting and give you feedback afterwards. Then, when you feel you have got the hang of the basics, you can start trying each time to ask the most useful version of that question that you can for the purpose at hand. Remember, too aggressive a use of questioning can make others feel under pressure, so be gentle with your practice.

Meanwhile, be on the lookout for magic questions that other people keep in their back pockets. My favourite question is: if you knew the answer, what would it be?

10 of Hearts – eye contact

The idea

John Heron, whom we have already met, also has a bee in his bonnet about eye contact. He has a wonderful exercise called 'phenomeno-logical gazing', where he encourages you to look deeply and at length into the eyes of someone well known to you. He suggests your wife, lover, long-standing friend or bank manager (!). Maybe practise on one of the first three first, because it is a very powerful exercise. Leadership is about connection, and one of the chief ways we connect is through eye contact. Eyes have always been considered the 'windows of the soul' so it can feel extremely exposing being fully beheld. Indeed, when you try this exercise, you will see the lengths to which we will go to avoid gaze. Heron likens this to a visit to the optician. One minute they are examining your eyes by looking at them, the next minute they are holding your gaze by looking into them. It feels qualitatively different, and we are more comfortable with the former. So, we get the giggles and fool around to break the tension, or we get curious about eye colour or make-up or spectacle frames. Eventually, we settle and we exchange gaze. In this moment, we learn what connection is and how seldom we encounter it. And once you feel confident being seen and beholding another, you learn to trust yourself again. You do not need to search the heavens for cues in the conversation – their eyes will tell you what you need to do, and you will not forget your lines if they are still the right ones to say.

The exercise

Good eye contact has a number of attendant virtues. Chiefly, it allows you to signal to colleagues that you have noticed them. This must not be gainsaid, because one of our deepest psychological needs is to feel significant, to feel seen. So next time a colleague interrupts you while you are typing, imagine they are a lip reader and can only hear you when you face them. Stop what you are doing and look at them. Apart from anything else, it is likely to make the interruption shorter, as they will not have to keep talking until they feel they have your full attention. Eye contact saves words. It allows you to use pauses with devastating impact. A bit like a radio presenter who is faced with dead air, being held by your gaze will make even the most robust colleague get quickly to the point or move swiftly on. So, improve your ability to connect with others by doing an eye contact audit. You do not need to stare everybody down; start simply by being more aware of when you hold gaze and when you tend to look away. Steady and interested eye contact shows confidence and engagement, and lets the person know they are important to you. If you feel that the intensity of direct eye contact would be inappropriate, use an old acting trick. To avoid blinking in close-ups, actors stare at the bridge of the person's nose instead. It looks the same. And if you want a sneaky reason to improve your eye contact, a 2007 study by psychologist Nora Murphy showed that people will perceive you to be more intelligent if you do. When you are more aware of your patterns in this regard, try giving the person you are with your full attention through eye contact, but remember to smile as well, so that they do not feel intimidated.

9 of Hearts – storytelling

The idea

Have you ever tried cheese and onion bread-and-butter pudding? I spent five weeks living in a monastery once. The Benedictine community at Douai Abbey pride themselves on their hospitality and the food was brilliant. I had fled there to escape myself, in order to write the theology chapter of my doctorate. It was quite a drastic move for an extrovert – even the meals were silent, so my poor husband would get a call every night during which I would just witter away in order to get some words out. My task was to summarize the whole of theology ever, because by then I had been so long in a business school environment that I had a notion there must be a 2x2 matrix for theology. There is, by the way. On my travels I discovered a brilliant book that does the same sort of thing for stories. Written by Christopher Booker, it is called *The Seven Basic Plots* and it was thirty-four years in the making. Just so you can have fun sorting all of your favourite books and movies into categories, the seven basic plots are: Overcoming the Monster, Rags to Riches, The Quest, Voyage and Return, Comedy, Tragedy, and Rebirth. Obviously sagas like *The Lord of the Rings* or *Star Wars* combine several of these themes to make their attraction even stronger.

Booker's interest in stories was sparked off by the realization that we are immersed in them, yet are uncommonly uncurious about them as a phenomenon. Vast parts of our day are taken up following stories, through social media, radio, television, office gossip, the news, books and the drama of everyday conversations. We dream in stories, too. From infancy we demand stories and the stories we tell our children – nursery rhymes, fairy tales, myths and legends – have been handed down to us through the generations. The wisdom traditions know this well and have preserved their teaching in stories too – lessons about good and evil, and about how we should live our lives. Stories have a unique capacity to spark our imagination and to engage our brains more fully than just a recounting of facts. The Canadian author Keith Oatley argues that stories run on the minds of readers just like computer simulations run on computers. While we listen to them, in some senses we live them, which is why they are so powerful. And now that we have the technology to peep into brains, we can use scanning to see that this is indeed true. Many more areas of the brain are involved when we hear a story, as opposed to a simple presentation of facts.

Here is one of my favourite stories about meaning and purpose at work:

A man is walking along a road and sees a stonemason working. He stops to admire the smooth blocks of stone and the stonemason stops working to have a break and pass the time of day. The man asks: 'What are you doing?' The stonemason answers: 'I come here every morning and work until nightfall cutting stones for my master.

It pays the bills. I can't complain.' The man bids him farewell and continues his journey. Further along the road, he meets another stonemason. This one is working flat out and has a much larger pile of stones beside him. The man asks: 'What are you doing?' The stonemason answers: 'Sorry, I can't stop to talk. I'm paid according to the number of stones I cut each day, so I must get on.' The man bids him farewell and continues his journey. Further along the road, he meets a third stonemason, who has an even larger and beautifully cut pile of stones beside him. The man asks: 'What are you doing?' The stonemason answers: 'I'm building a cathedral.'

The exercise

We all tell stories by accident, but lack confidence about our storytelling ability when we are asked to produce one on the spur of the moment. That is why Christmas stockings are stuffed full of books of anecdotes for after-dinner or best-man speeches. The brilliant leader has the knack of throwing stories into the conversation, as a way of communicating complex messages in a simple, engaging and memorable way, so it is a vital skill of the craft. I get the leaders I know to practise with props – to find a physical metaphor for what it is they are trying to say. Equally you can use a strong visual which conjures up a story, or start with an anecdote that indicates what you want your audience to take away from what they have heard. Like so many of the skills we have discussed here, though, the best way is to learn from the masters. Seek out those people around you who are good at spinning yarns. Watch what they do and copy them. And plunder kind Aunt Mildred's stocking filler for ideas.

8 of Hearts – relationships

The idea

One way of defining 'sustainability' is about the health of each relationship we have – with each other, with our communities, with society, with the planet, and inter-generationally. Our species has survived largely because we co-operate with each other. Being altruistic and helpful to others is rewarded in our bodies through the release of oxytocin and the stimulation of the para-sympathetic nervous system. We are hard-wired to receive positive feedback when we co-operate, to encourage this behaviour in the future. Similarly, if we are lonely, a group of neurons in our dorsal raphe nucleus drives us out to seek company, because we are biologically in danger if we are isolated. We do not relate to each other because we want to get something out of it, we relate to each other because that is what we are programmed to do.

At work, our ability to relate as well as we normally do in our private lives has been interrupted by interference. This noise is partly to do with power and politics, but also to do with the prevailing work narrative of competition, which suggests that life in business is a zero-sum game and one we must be sure to win. The playing of games in general is a rich source of data, as we know from formal game theory. But so is the evolution of board games. Stewart Woods did his PhD on eurogames at Curtin University in Perth, Australia. A eurogame is a German-style board game that emphasizes strategy, downplays luck and conflict, and keeps all the players in the game until it ends. You are playing against the game itself more than you are playing against your opponents. They are a genre apart from the likes of Monopoly, which goes on for hours and is about annihilating your opponents in order to win. Eurogames are sociable and designed to keep everyone in play for as long as possible, with balancing mechanisms integrated into the rules to advantage lagging players and hinder the leaders. This keeps it competitive to the very end. And these games have a lesson for relationships at work. We need colleagues, so we should nurture them, so that we all make it to the end of the game in one piece. We should be playing the ball, not the man. And we should be playing against ourselves and the task in hand, not against each other.

It is also generally in our job description to help our colleagues, so we might as well get on with it. It will also boost employee engagement and earn you more discretionary effort from those around you.

The exercise

Plot your relationships at work. Get a large piece of paper and coloured pencils and draw a small circle in the middle with your name inside it. Then draw your web of work relationships, giving each person their own circle. Now pay attention to the connectors between you and each person. Code each relationship Red/Amber/Green. How could you improve those that are red or amber? Are you doing enough to maintain the greens? Are there any missing relationships that you ought to cultivate for the future or which might help with existing relationships that are strained?

Next, look at each relationship again. Highlight the colleagues with whom you work most closely. For each of them, write down what you think they need from you and code them Red/Amber/Green again, for the extent to which you think you meet this need for them. For the reds, what could you do to improve your ability to meet this need? Diary in any actions you could take that would help. If you are feeling brave, ask these colleagues directly what they need from you, perhaps as preparation for your appraisal or objective-setting process, or during theirs. And ask them how well you are doing and how you could meet their needs better. Do your lists match what you hear from them directly?

As insurance for the future, you may as well follow the advice of the American writer Anne Herbert: practice random kindness and senseless acts of beauty. It will cheer you up no end.

7 of Hearts – choreographed conversations

The idea

John Heron, again, is my guru of choice on well-choreographed conversations, because he has studied them in detail as a vital tool of the trade for any professional working with a client. His model is rather similar to Daniel Goleman's 'golf clubs' model on style, so you will recognize the contrast between 'push' and 'pull'. I am using it here because it was devised specifically for the choreographing of elegant conversations, particularly those designed to be of help to your conversation partner, in a work setting. Given that all of my heart cards are about manners, this altruistic intent appeals. Even better, this tool works for 1:1s and it works as a facilitation tool, so that you can use it to steer group discussions, too.

Heron calls his push styles 'authoritative interventions' and his pull ones 'facilitative interventions'. He has three styles for each. His premise is that a good conversationalist will regard these six as the basic dance steps which, when mastered and combined, will produce the full variety of dances that any conversation may require.

The push styles are:

1 Prescribing – telling someone what to do
2 Informing – providing information or options
3 Confronting – holding a mirror up, either positively or negatively

The pull styles are:

1 Cathartic – releasing emotions that may be blocking progress
2 Catalytic – asking questions to speed the thinking process along
3 Supporting – expressing solidarity and support

You may be able to spot some of these manoeuvres now. 'You could do A or B, but I always find that A works best – let me know if you need a hand with it.' This conversation comprises informing, prescribing, then supporting. 'I heard some great feedback about you the other day. People think you are A and B. Why don't you try for that promotion now?' A combination of confronting, informing, prescribing. 'You seem upset. How can I help?' A cathartic and catalytic intervention. So the dance need not be long, just expertly constructed. Equally you can use this approach to programme a lengthier interaction, perhaps a coaching conversation, or a conversation about priorities or difficulties.

The exercise

Again, to improve your skill in this area, start with meeting bingo to see how good you are at identifying the full range of interventions. If any are neglected, you might want to add them into the discussion. When you feel confident, start noticing your own habits and patterns and gently vary them to increase your range. Some you will find easier than others, but knowing you have ready access to them all will help you feel that you have more choice in the conversations you have, and more options at your disposal if the conversation does not go the way you planned.

6 of Hearts – coaching

The idea

While at Deloitte, I had the enormous privilege of being trained in coaching by the legendary Sir John Whitmore. His course took two days, in which all we did was ask each other a lot of questions. Sir John likes questions. He separates them out into 'selfish' questions, which could be solved with a Vulcan mind-meld, and 'learner-focused' questions, which create new insight because they expand the learner's understanding of the issue they face. You get very good at scoring everyone else's questions out of ten. A really insightful question will have your colleague squirming in their chair, saying 'Oh, good question' and finding it really hard to come up with an answer without considerable thought. Rubbish questions are answered instantly and inspire a 'yes, but ...' dance which frustrates everyone involved.

For Sir John, coaching is fundamentally about *awareness* and *responsibility*. To promote these aims, he devised the famous GROW model. In introducing it, he worries that we assume junior colleagues are like empty buckets, just waiting to be filled by our regurgitated wisdom, which he charmingly terms 'managers' effluent'. He prefers GROW because it reminds him of oak trees and acorns. He thinks that people are more like acorns than buckets. You do not need to dig an acorn up every five minutes to ask it how it is growing. You just plant it in an auspicious place, protect the site, and ensure it has the necessary conditions to thrive.

GROW stands for Goal, Reality, Options and Will. The conversation may start with any of these items, but will need to have covered all of them to work well. First, Goal. This is the asking of lots of questions designed to set or clarify the goal for the learning project in general or for this particular conversation. Second, Reality, which involves lots of questions to solicit a really thorough awareness of the situation right now. Third, Options – the finding of alternative strategies, solutions and answers. Lastly, Will – the testing of your commitment to your goal, and the confirming of your concrete, realistic plans to reach it.

The exercise

Coaching is the best way to demonstrate an interest in others and to check your understanding of their situation. It also teaches them to self-coach over time. So next time colleagues raise problems with you, do not just offer your knee-jerk advice. Instead, ask them questions. Could they say more about the problem? Could they say what they have already tried to do about it and what this has taught them? How are they feeling about it? What kind of help do they want? Who else might have solved a similar problem in the past? Where else might they go for help? What you could do that might help them? Remember, this approach works best if you combine it with excellent listening, which might include summarizing, reflecting back and probing, but seldom interrupting. They will feel invested in and you will have fewer problems to solve over time.

With the kind permission of Sir John, here as Table 11 is a short version of the tool so you can try it yourself. You could start by applying it to a problem you currently face to test it out.

Also at finishing school, they taught me how to walk. Feet at 10 to 2, heels never straying far from the line of masking tape running ahead across the floor. It was important, they said, for us to master the standard walk. Then, we were told, we could 'add personality' to it.

Similarly, this tool works well if it is not a straitjacket. However, limbering up with a process of simple questions stops you from sneaking in premature advice and solutions. Once you feel confident that you can make the right calls in the conversation, you can 'add personality' back in.

Table 11 GROW

Goal	What exactly do you want to achieve?
	What measures could you use to track progress?
	How much of it is within your own control?
	How will you know you have achieved it?
	How well are you doing now, on a scale of 1–10?
Reality	What have you done so far to move towards this goal?
	What have you learned from that?
	Are there any constraints, other than you, that stop you achieving it?
	How might you overcome them?
	What are the reasons for the score you gave yourself above?
	Are there any people or situations that affect this score either way?
	What is really stopping you?
Options	What could you do to move towards this goal?
	What else could you do?
	What else could you do?
	What else could you do?
	If time was not a factor, what could you do?
	If money was not a factor, what could you do?
	What will happen if you do nothing?
	Who does this well and what do they do that you could try?
Will	Which of the options will you choose?
	Who else needs to help and support you in your plan?
	What obstacles do you expect to meet?
	How will you overcome them?
	On what day and at what time will you take your first step?
	And what is your level of commitment to achieving this goal, out of 10?
	If it is less than 8, how could you improve this score?

5 of Hearts – teams

The idea

I have a hunch about teams. A lot of time, effort and budget is spent on team-building, but I think the reason leaders struggle with it is: (a) they really do think it is quicker to do everything themselves; and (b) they are hoping that any variability in team performance will be ironed out by the peer pressure of an off-site, so that they do not have to have any difficult conversations themselves.

Yes, you are right, it is almost always quicker to do it yourself. In the short term. But it is not wise. And you may or may not like teams. But your ability to deliver results through them will only get more important the more senior you get. So you may as well establish a reputation for being brilliant at teams sooner rather than later, if only as a hedge against your future career.

The exercise

And there are various tried and tested ways to improve your bravery around teams. You could try team-building in the outdoors or you could use psychometric tools to learn more about your differences as a team. But for you personally, the best way to start growing your abilities in this area is just to do it more. Is there anything you are currently working on by yourself that would lend itself to being done by a small team? Perhaps there is something you are loath to delegate, but if it were done by several colleagues, reporting to you, you would feel more comfortable? It might be slower, it might be less good, but if your parents had tied your shoelaces for you every day you would never have learned how to do it for yourself. So do not be selfish. Invest in the development of those around you and it will honour you.

And if there is anything patchy about your team, do not just throw a psychometric at it to make the point about gaps. Address any unhelpful behaviours privately head-on and take the plank out of your own eye before you look for the splinters in theirs. What shifts could you make in your own patterns or behaviours that would create a shift in the team culture? Could you vary tasks, accountability, reporting, location, anything else? If goals are shared and clear; you have a healthy feedback culture; and you pay attention to the development of 'colleague' skills like listening and coaching, excellent teams simply emerge.

4 of Hearts – feedback

The idea

When I was at Deloitte and a Partner fixed you with his beady eye and barked 'Feedback – offline!', your knees started to knock. I gather the culture at Apple was similar, if more public, and someone I know at Tesco once had his carefully written report torn in two by Sir Terry at a board meeting and was told 'there's your feedback'. This *Apprentice*-style approach seems only to be on the rise. But why does feedback have to be such a negative experience?

I once watched a training exercise where two volunteers were sent out of the room. When the first one walked back into the room, the crowd had to get them to write their name on a flip chart, solely through the use of booing and jeering if they put a foot wrong. After ten minutes or so, they froze to the spot, scared that any move would produce a negative response. The exercise was then repeated with the second volunteer, only this time the crowd had to applaud and cheer if the subject made a move that would contribute towards the goal. It took this person only a few minutes to achieve the task. Simplistic perhaps, but this exercise sums up years of research into negative incentives.

Packaging feedback is tricky, especially if the message may be negatively received. Everyone can now see the traditional 'stroke-kick-stroke' package coming a mile off. Giving good quality positive and negative feedback is both a gift and a skill. The most common way in which we undermine this competence is our wish to be nice. We want to be liked and to avoid conflict, so we pull our punches, in case speaking truth to power becomes career-limiting. The best way to flex this muscle is to improve your feedback skills. If you are unfeignedly honest with those around you, they learn that it is not only acceptable but they learn the value of it too. How are we ever to improve if we do not know how we are doing? Whichever tool or model you use, please apply it without destroying the vulnerable people around you. In the workplace we may be getting ever better at pretending we are tough, but no one likes abuse. One of the most unforgivable facets of modern management is the requirement to subject yourself to your boss's feedback, no matter how poorly it is given. Indeed, we seem to be encouraging bad bosses at the moment, in the mistaken belief that personality flaws are the price you pay for brilliance. Work by Mary Jacobsen suggests that this is absolutely not the case. Because it offends against our ideas of equity that some people should just be more gifted than others, we compensate by assigning them – in life as in literature and in movies – personality flaws, and imagining they are socially inadequate. This may be the case where a gifted person owes that giftedness to autism or psychopathy, but these are exceptions. The truly talented literally use more of their brains than the rest of us, including their emotional and social faculties, so this myth is not accurate, even if it makes us feel better. So, let us stop accepting poorly given feedback, by offering immediate feedback on the feedback, to help the giver to recast their message in a way that is actually helpful, by the use of careful questions. This takes guts – and practice – but the more we can create cultures of elegance in this art, the more we will all improve.

The exercise

One of the models we use at Ashridge is the BOFF model: Behaviour, Outcome, Feelings, Future. You can use it positively or critically.

> When you stepped up to the flip chart in that meeting and summarized our discussion so succinctly, it really helped move the discussion on. I felt hugely relieved and could see everyone else relaxing as they realized that we might just get out of here by lunchtime. I wonder if you might consider doing this more in future? It was really valuable.

Or,

> I noticed that when you cut John off in the meeting and told him his idea would never work, it shut him up for the rest of the meeting. I am really worried that the more junior members of the team will not now want to risk upsetting you by speaking out. Perhaps next time you could ask others for their reaction before giving yours, and perhaps you could frame your criticisms more positively?

My advice would be to build up a stock of positive 'BOFFs' before you start the more challenging ones. That way, you build your skill and confidence in feedback-giving, as well as your bank of credit for being more critical in future. And honesty about just how good someone is could arguably be more powerful than the reverse. I would also advise the reluctant feedback-giver to get into the habit of giving feedback to anyone, not just to direct reports; and whenever a behaviour is notable, not just at appraisal time. Some companies are now getting rid of appraisals altogether – you do not need them if you have a robust feedback culture. So who could you give some feedback to today?

3 of Hearts – thank yous

The idea
For some reason I grew up with the belief that you do not really own a present or have the right to use it until you have dispatched the thank-you letter for it. It was certainly an effective strategy on the part of my parents to keep me glued to my thank-you letters instead of the TV on Christmas afternoon. While I am slowly weaning myself off this rather extreme view, it is actually good training. Thanking is feedback. If an effort is made and it disappears into a vacuum, the person who made it has no idea whether the effort was worth making. So they may not repeat the effort in the future. And while this is no substitute for good disciplines around feedback more generally, a simple thank-you helps to encourage repeat performance in the future. This insight is crucial in organizations, because there will always be a boss or two who never seems to notice. But if their colleagues lose heart, the whole organization suffers. So you can do the thanking for them, to keep spirits up.

The exercise
Appoint yourself the local cheerleader. Depending on your personal style, this could just be about firing off quick emails to congratulate colleagues on a good meeting or presentation. Or it could be about old-fashioned thank-you cards. Or playful gifts like sweets or biscuits to let people know that you have noticed and appreciated their work.

If you have a good calendar system, remembering birthdays is a gentle way to show appreciation, if you just need an opportunity for a more general thank-you. One chief executive surprises staff with an 'unbirthday' which is a great way to recognize their contribution. So buy some stamps and a box of postcards and send one a week.

And yes, as usual, there are selfish reasons to be thankful, because gratitude is good for you. Robert Emmons has written a book called *Thanks* which explains why being grateful boosts life satisfaction, vitality, happiness, self-esteem, optimism, hope and empathy. Which is quite a list. On the downside, being ungrateful leads to anxiety, depression, envy, materialism and loneliness. Not good. So what works best? In all the research into happiness, one core practice stands out: count your blessings. If you do so, regularly, you will be on average 25 per cent happier than those who do not, and this happiness will be sustained over time. With my twins at bedtime we do 'sorrys and thank-yous'. You probably did some kind of bedtime ritual with your own parents. But nowadays we are so exhausted we fall into bed without pausing first to review the day, until insomnia kicks in and we wake up worrying instead. So, could you try just briefly as you fall asleep to notice the gifts your day has brought? Better still, write them down before you turn out the lights, because making the process as concrete as possible cements the benefits of doing it. Emmons' studies found that it helps you sleep better, too.

2 of Hearts – character

The idea

We have discussed the importance of character earlier on in the book. Specifically, we have looked at the crucial importance of keeping the virtues exercised so that they remain supple and ready for use. But which virtues do we mean? Down the centuries we have been given a number of lists, like the traditional seven: prudence, justice, temperance, courage, faith, hope and charity. More recently, when the UK Department for Education launched its initiative to promote the teaching of character in schools, they defined character as the traits, attributes and behaviours that underpin success in both education and work. They listed these as:

perseverance, resilience and grit; confidence and optimism; motivation, drive and ambition; neighbourliness and community spirit; tolerance and respect; honesty, integrity and dignity; conscientiousness, curiosity and focus.

Although this list is focused on school-age formation, the read across to leadership is striking. Whichever list you prefer, you probably know which of your own virtues need the most work. But how can you do this, exactly?

I recall my first-ever job interview, in the Establishment office at the Church Commissioners in Westminster, London. While puffing merrily on a cigarette, my interviewer asked me: if the angels offered you a virtue, which one would you choose? I said 'patience'. While I wait for the angels to arrive, how might I develop this virtue on my own? By waiting, deliberately. By noticing how cross I get when my computer takes ages to come on, or someone puts me on hold, or a long queue has formed. Children find waiting terribly hard. So we have advent candles for them, to help them wait patiently for Christmas. Every day, we light the candle and watch it burn away another number. Advent calendars used to work, too, until we packed them full of chocolate for instant gratification. The candle, though, is a great discipline.

What do you find it hard to wait for? Or who tries your patience the most? A friend of mine who went to a convent school remembers a nun who, instead of swearing at the children, would exclaim: 'St JUDE preserve us!' It was only when my friend was older she realized that St Jude was the patron saint of lost causes. This is actually a cunningly disguised way of practising patience, and a similar manoeuvre to the 'counting to ten' that we have seen before. Is there someone particularly annoying you could make the target of your practice, so that you gradually increase your tolerance of them, as a way of strengthening this virtue? Or could you develop your own version of a candle to help you with your waiting?

The exercise

You can apply my patience example to any of your virtues that need some work. But you might like to start by thinking about how your character has already been developed. This is important because it shows you that you have already proved your resilience. You just need to be confident enough about how you deployed your resilience to know that you can do so again in the future. To start answering this question, identify your crucible moments. When in your life has your mettle really been tested? Your strength, your generosity, your patience, your humility – any virtues you notice were the residue left after the flames burned away. One way to find them is to think about medals. I am short, so when I attend military events, I am eye height with a lot of them. Imagine you have received several medals during the course of your leadership career for your courage or bravery. What were they awarded for? What did these events teach you?

Or perhaps you learned virtue more slowly, from key people in your life who instilled in you by their example a deep commitment to love, friendship, loyalty, determination, quality – any characteristic you admire and are pleased you possess. These reflections should be giving you an emerging inventory of the virtues your life has wrought in you. But are there gaps or virtues that are in abeyance? Looking forwards, are there virtues you fear you will increasingly need, but that do not yet feel reliable? Who could you learn these from, or what small tests could you introduce into your life to practise them?

Conclusion

Creating your own on-the-job simulation

This book has looked at an empirically tested list of the kinds of things that a leadersmith would do well to learn. Each Critical Incident is mapped to the key practices you will need to navigate them: your winning hands (see Appendix 1). But your particular career may not readily fit this recipe, which you will need to tailor to suit you. The best way to figure out how, is to schedule in some strategic job shadowing. You can start this process by writing four lists:

1 jobs you would love to do in the future;
2 your leadership role models;
3 jobs you are terrified of, because you know nothing about them; and
4 jobs in your organization or sector you ought to know more about.

There is a template for this in Appendix 4. Are there any overlaps? Who in any of these fields could you spend a day with? Or do you just have some extraordinary friends you could wild-card job-shadow?

What emerges will show you where you have gaps, or where your next learning threshold might be. My invitation would be for you to include on your agenda all of those Critical Incidents that would otherwise keep you awake at night in future and schedule them in now. On your time, in your territory, so that you can manage the risk of unleashing yourself upon them. Perhaps they are versions of some of the Critical Incidents we have met here. Perhaps they are new ones. The same principles apply – templating now will resource you to deal with them better next time. Meanwhile, what follows now are some final thoughts for your journey.

Pressure

The approach suggested in this book is about collecting useful templates for the future. I imagine if you know that the showpiece for *The Great British Bake Off* is a soufflé, or that the dance you are doing for *Strictly* is a tango, you do something similar – you get very familiar with a whole range of versions of the ideal so that you can develop your own approach. Then all you need to do is cope with your nerves and adjust your recipe in the light of what you encounter on the day. While in these instances and in traditional apprenticing, you can take your time and build up your expertise slowly and in modules, I am suggesting that with leading you can also jump-start your prowess by using pressure. Pressure, not only because it helps you learn better in the moment, but because it gives you a better memory of the experience for the future. But templating under pressure is a dangerous game if you do not take care of yourself properly.

Famously, it is music stars who trash their guitars and hotel rooms after performances, or indulge in high-risk behaviours to 'come down' after a gig. The police are always on red-alert after football matches for similar reasons, because domestic violence soars when disappointed fans get home. This wholly negative externalizing of the adrenaline that has built up is a warning.

In a pressure situation, through the proverbial 'fight-or-flight' reaction, our bodies prepare us for physical exertion. The physical act of fighting or fleeing would also metabolize the stress hormones produced. But if we have no outlet for this chemical surge, it will either burst out through violence or lurk internally un-metabolized. Cortisol, for example, deliberately increases blood pressure and blood sugar to help you physically in an emergency situation. It temporarily suppresses the immune system so you can focus on survival. But leaving stress hormones like cortisol in the body longer-term means that these temporary measures start turning against you, by keeping your blood pressure and blood sugar levels raised and suppressing your ability to resist infection and heal longer-term. Burn-out results, together with symptoms of insomnia, anxiety, stress, heart attacks and diabetes, as your body starts using up body chemistry and running on empty. And while in the short term cortisol will boost your memory, in the longer term it will start inhibiting both your learning and your ability to retrieve memories.

As a discipline, every time you feel your heart rate increase, you must help it back down. Your body does this by deploying the parasympathetic nervous system, to return you to the 'rest and digest' state. You can assist at a very efficient and physical level by immediately exercising, metabolizing your stress hormones by a simulated fight or flight. Even running up the stairs will do, if you would otherwise have to wait before you can do more formal cardio-vascular exercise. Less physically, the parasympathetic nervous system is also stimulated by acts of kindness, through nurture or charity. Coaching, music, singing, dancing, laughing, looking after plants, animals or children – all of these have been shown to help, as has the ingesting of the omega-3 fatty acids found in fish oils, walnuts and flaxseed. Caffeine and alcohol do not help though, so try to minimize your intake, particularly when you need to optimize your energy.

There are many elite athletes, actors, musicians and performers who have had to get professionally expert at managing these peaks and troughs. If they are well managed, high performance can continue throughout an illustrious career, If not, stars shoot up like rockets but fall quickly back down to earth. It might be the stuff of legend to go out in a blaze of glory, but it is a risky career strategy and is deeply unfair on those who love you. So do not be an idiot about it. It is efficient to learn under pressure, because you do not want to waste any time. So do not then waste the time you have won for yourself by making yourself ill. You are too precious and the world needs your leadership.

Transparency

I made the bold claim earlier in the book that the essence of leading does not change radically over time. I truly believe this. But one thing that will shift in our lifetime is the environment in which leaders have to lead. For me, this will be characterized by radical transparency. Societal changes that are reducing the power distance in organizations means more empowered staff, who want to play a role and to share responsibility for the future of their workplace. The new ubiquity of social media makes whistle-blowing reflexive, so there is nowhere to hide if your products, services, governance, or supply chain disappoints. And boards, carrying increasingly onerous regulatory burdens, will not just want to be fed party lines either. Leaders will feel ever more exposed to scrutiny from all sides at once. And the only way to cope with this is to be wholly transparent. This carries acute political risk.

It should be said that this will feel worse for men. As you may know, under pressure men are biologically programmed to adopt a zero-sum game mentality and to try to win at all costs. This helped our survival as a species when the sabre-toothed tigers were in town. Information is power, so old habits about 'playing your cards close to your chest' become instinctive. Women, however, primed in conflict by oxytocin, have a more affiliative reaction, which makes them want to communicate and share. Again, useful when our job was to keep the home fires burning. And, in a world where playing games with information makes you arguably more vulnerable, this female instinct will prove more useful. So feed your instincts to communicate, because they are likely to be right.

Legacy

In our original research, many leaders told us about the delight they felt when colleagues they were coaching did well. Partly as a virtuous discipline, and partly to cement your own learning, a vital element of your leadersmithing will be to become an apprentice master to others. This may be part of your formal line management role, but if you do not have staff, you can develop other colleagues in your sector or network anyway. The beauty of a template approach is that your own experience will show you where you might encourage more junior colleagues to search out their own Critical Incidents. And, having yourself survived them, you will have great radar about how best to calibrate the level of risk for your colleagues. Can you develop your own list of what you know now that you wish you had known ten years ago, so you can share it with them? Looking into the future, I would love to see more organizations formalizing the role of their senior cadre in this way. With longevity making it likely that we will all be working into our seventies, what a legacy it would be if we could have senior colleagues spend their last seven years apprenticing junior colleagues into the tradecraft of leading.

Art and mystery?

The current Archbishop of York has a lovely story about camels. There once was a Bedouin who had three sons and seventeen camels. In his will, he left half of his seventeen camels to his elder son, one-third to his second son and one-ninth to his youngest son. When the father died, the children attempted to divide the camels according to their father's will and struggled to divide seventeen camels into one-half, one-third and one-ninth. They went to consult a very wise old man, who said: 'Simple. I will lend you my camel. It will be the eighteenth and you can get what your father wanted you to have.' Eureka! Half of eighteen is nine, a third of eighteen is six and a ninth of eighteen is two, making a total of seventeen. The sons divided up the camels, then the wise old man took his camel home. Likewise, a good leader knows that they are essentially a catalyst to help complex things work out smoothly. Your vocation is always to be the eighteenth camel.

The Wizard of Oz

Even though they knew the Wizard of Oz had no power, the Scarecrow, the Tin Man and Lion still believed that he had made them smart, loving and brave. Who would need to tell you that you were all of these things for you to believe it? Remember, you do not need to be smart, loving and brave, you just need to feel as though you are. Feeling resourced to meet challenges means that you will be able to do so in reality. Having the tradecraft of the leadersmith at your fingertips will give you a steady confidence that you can master anything.

One refrain that came out time and time again from leaders answering our question about what they wish they had known ten years ago was: 'I wish I'd known that I can do it.' Well, you can. I hope this book gives you some ideas about how you can convince yourself and those around you that you have what it takes. Tomorrow, do not be the best leader. Do not even try to be a good one. Just be better.

Leadersmithing takes a lifetime – so be a tortoise, not a hare.

Appendix 1

Table 12 lays out a set of winning hands for each of the seventeen Critical Incidents. This is not to say that other cards could not be played, and the hands vary in length. But these would be my priority cards in each case, and you may want to use them as a starting point for planning your preparation.

Table 12 Preparing for Critical Incidents – the winning hands

Critical Incident	Winning Hand	
Stepping up	A♦	Your Strengths
	7♦	Composure
	5♦	Initiative
	J♠	Conflict
	8♠	Communication
	4♠	Working the Room
	K♣	Sleep
	Q♣	Fuel
	7♣	Control
	6♣	Gravitas
	5♣	Posture
	10♥	Eye Contact
	2♥	Character
Taking key decisions	K♦	Effort
	Q♦	Uncertainty
	5♦	Initiative
	K♠	Numbers
	Q♠	Creativity
	J♠	Conflict
	2♠	MECE
	K♣	Sleep
	Q♣	Fuel
	2♥	Character
Coping with increasing change	K♦	Effort
	9♦	Attention
	6♦	Hope
	8♠	Communication
	10♣	Change
	K♥	Trust

Critical Incident	Winning Hand	
Managing ambiguity	Q♦	Uncertainty
	J♦	Letting Go
	10♦	Improvisation
	8♦	Mood
	6♦	Hope
	8♠	Communication
	J♣	Personal Brand
	8♣	Power
	7♣	Control
	K♥	Trust
Taking a risk	Q♦	Uncertainty
	6♦	Hope
	5♦	Initiative
	A♠	Difficult Conversations
	K♠	Numbers
	Q♠	Creativity
	9♠	Delegation
	3♠	Mystery Shopping
	K♥	Trust
	2♥	Character
Accepting when you get it wrong	K♦	Effort
	J♦	Letting Go
	8♦	Mood
	7♦	Composure
	6♦	Hope
	A♣	Work–Life Balance
	K♣	Sleep
	2♥	Character
Key board/stakeholder meeting	7♦	Composure
	A♠	Difficult Conversations
	K♠	Numbers
	7♠	Public Speaking
	5♣	Posture
	4♣	Sumptuary Law
	K♥	Trust
	Q♥	Listening
	10♥	Eye Contact
	9♥	Storytelling

Critical Incident	Winning Hand	
Doing the maths	9♦	Attention
	K♠	Numbers
	Q♠	Creativity
	8♠	Communication
	5♠	Networking
	3♠	Mystery Shopping
	J♥	Questions
	9♥	Storytelling
Joining the dots	K♠	Numbers
	8♠	Communication
	5♠	Networking
	3♠	Mystery Shopping
	9♣	Reading Cultures
	Q♥	Listening
	9♥	Storytelling
	8♥	Relationships
Motivating and influencing others	10♦	Improvisation
	6♦	Hope
	9♠	Delegation
	3♣	Colours
	A♥	Manners
	Q♥	Listening
	J♥	Questions
	10♥	Eye Contact
	9♥	Storytelling
	7♥	Choreographed Conversations
	6♥	Coaching
	4♥	Feedback
	3♥	Thank Yous
Flexing style	K♦	Effort
	4♦	Habits
	3♦	Missing Person
	6♠	Meetings
	J♣	Personal Brand
	9♣	Reading Cultures
	Q♥	Listening
	8♥	Relationships
	7♥	Choreographed Conversations
	6♥	Coaching

Critical Incident	Winning Hand	
Delegating to and empowering staff	J♦	Letting Go
	6♦	Hope
	10♠	Remaining Competitive
	9♠	Delegation
	J♥	Questions
	8♥	Relationships
	7♥	Choreographed Conversations
	6♥	Coaching
	5♥	Teams
	4♥	Feedback
Dealing with poor performance	7♦	Composure
	A♠	Difficult Conversations
	J♠	Conflict
	K♥	Trust
	Q♥	Listening
	10♥	Eye Contact
	7♥	Choreographed Conversations
	6♥	Coaching
	4♥	Feedback
	2♥	Character
Listening to staff	9♦	Attention
	6♠	Meetings
	9♣	Reading Cultures
	2♣	Social Media
	A♥	Manners
	K♥	Trust
	Q♥	Listening
	10♥	Eye Contact
	8♥	Relationships
	4♥	Feedback
Knowing when to seek help and advice	A♦	Your Strengths
	4♦	Habits
	3♦	Missing Person
	2♦	Role Models
	10♠	Remaining Competitive
	5♠	Networking
	8♣	Power
	4♥	Feedback

Critical Incident	Winning Hand	
Giving and taking feedback	9♦	Attention
	4♦	Habits
	A♠	Difficult Conversations
	A♥	Manners
	Q♥	Listening
	10♥	Eye Contact
	8♥	Relationships
	7♥	Choreographed Conversations
	6♥	Coaching
	4♥	Feedback
Work–life balance	J♦	Letting Go
	8♦	Mood
	7♦	Composure
	4♦	Habits
	2♦	Role Models
	A♣	Work–Life Balance
	K♣	Sleep
	Q♣	Fuel
	A♠	Difficult Conversations
	10♠	Remaining Competitive

Appendix 2

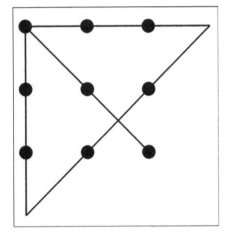

Figure 7 The nine-dot puzzle solved

Appendix 3

For each item in the table, award yourself a Red for under-resourced, an Amber for OK and a Green for well-resourced (RAG). Looking at your diary, when is your next opportunity to practise this skill?

Table 13 Self-assessment

Diamonds		RAG	Next chance to practise
A♦	Your Strengths		
K♦	Effort		
Q♦	Uncertainty		
J♦	Letting Go		
10♦	Improvisation		
9♦	Attention		
8♦	Mood		
7♦	Composure		
6♦	Hope		
5♦	Initiative		
4♦	Habits		
3♦	Missing Person		
2♦	Role Models		
Clubs		**RAG**	**Next chance to practise**
A♣	Work–Life Balance		
K♣	Sleep		
Q♣	Fuel		
J♣	Personal Brand		
10♣	Change		
9♣	Reading Cultures		
8♣	Power		
7♣	Control		
6♣	Gravitas		
5♣	Posture		
4♣	Sumptuary Law		
3♣	Colours		
2♣	Social Media		

Spades		RAG	Next chance to practise
A♠	Difficult Conversations		
K♠	Numbers		
Q♠	Creativity		
J♠	Conflict		
10♠	Remaining Competitive		
9♠	Delegation		
8♠	Communication		
7♠	Public Speaking		
6♠	Meetings		
5♠	Networking		
4♠	Working the Room		
3♠	Mystery Shopping		
2♠	MECE		
Hearts		**RAG**	**Next chance to practise**
A♥	Manners		
K♥	Trust		
Q♥	Listening		
J♥	Questions		
10♥	Eye Contact		
9♥	Storytelling		
8♥	Relationships		
7♥	Choreographed Conversations		
6♥	Coaching		
5♥	Teams		
4♥	Feedback		
3♥	Thank Yous		
2♥	Character		

Appendix 4

Table 14 Creating your own on-the-job simulation

Jobs I want to do in the future	Jobs I want but which terrify me
My role models	Jobs I need to know more about
Job shadowing opportunities	
What do these leaders know now that they wish they had known ten years ago?	
Which of these Critical Incidents could I schedule in now?	

Appendix 5

Book group questions

You may wish to use this book with your workplace book group or in another professional development setting. The following questions are merely suggestions. Alternatives might be simply to pick cards to discuss, or to challenge the whole group to try something out and report back at your next meeting.

1   What do you know now about yourself as a leader that you wish you had known ten years ago?
2   How did you learn it?
3   What do you think you will wish you had known, ten years hence?
4   How might you arrange to learn that early?
5   If leadersmithing is primarily about craft and apprentice pieces, looking at the work activities you have in prospect, could you turn any of them into apprentice pieces?
6   Is there anything you still need to master to be a fully confident leader? How could you start learning it now?
7   Which card could you pick to work on next week?

Bibliography

Ariely, Dan (2009), *Predictably Irrational* (London: HarperCollins).

Arthur, J., Kristjansson, K., Walker, D., Sanderse, W., Jones, C., Thoma, S., Curren, R. and Roberts, M. (2015), 'Character Education in UK Schools' (Birmingham: Jubilee Centre). Available online: http://www.jubileecentre.ac.uk/userfiles/jubileecentre/pdf/Research%20Reports/Character_Education_in_UK_Schools.pdf (accessed 30 June 2016).

Aslam, Mubeen M. (2006), 'Are You Selling the Right Colour? A Cross-cultural Review of Colour as a Marketing Cue', *Journal of Marketing Communications* 12 (1): 15–30.

Ayres, James (2014), *Art, Artisans & Apprentices* (Oxford: Oxbow).

Bacon, Lauren (2014), 'Your Work–Life Balance Hangs in these Four Quadrants'. Available online: http://qz.com/173703/your-work-life-balance-hangs-in-these-four-quadrants/ (accessed 30 June 2016).

Biggar, Nigel (2009), 'Saving the "Secular" – the Public Vocation of Moral Theology', *Journal of Religious Ethics* 37 (1).

Birdwell, J., Scott, R., Reynolds, L. (2015), 'Character Nation' (London, Demos). Available online: http://www.demos.co.uk/wp-content/uploads/2015/09/476_1505_characternation_web.pdf (accessed 30 June 2016).

Blascovich, J, and Tomaka, J (1996), 'The Biopsychosocial Model of Arousal Regulation', in P. M. Zanna (ed.). *Advances in Experimental Social Psychology*, vol. 28, 1–51 (San Diego, CA: Academic Press).

Bolchover, David (2005), *The Living Dead* (Chichester: Capstone).

Booker, Christopher (2004), *The Seven Basic Plots* (London: Continuum).

Breheny, Kathryn (2010), 'The Effect of Arousal On Reading Comprehension and Their Relationship With Heart-Rate Variability'. Unpublished thesis submitted for MSc in Research Methods in Psychology, Reading University.

Brooks, David (2015), *The Road to Character* (London: Allen Lane).

Buchanan, T. W. (2007), 'Retrieval of Emotional Memories', *Psychological Bulletin* 133: 761–79.

Buckingham, M. and Coffman, C. (1999), *First, Break All The Rules* (New York: Simon & Schuster).

Burkeman, Oliver (2011), *HELP!* (Edinburgh: Canongate).

Burkeman, Oliver (2013), *The Antidote* (Edinburgh: Canongate).

Cahill, L. and McGaugh, J. L. (1998), 'Mechanisms of Emotional Arousal and Lasting Declarative Memory', *Trends in Neurosciences* 21: 294–9.

Cattell, R. B. (1950), *Personality* (New York: McGraw Hill).

Clayton, Lucie (1968), *The World of Modelling* (London: George G. Harrap & Co. Ltd).

Coles, Bill (2013), *Red Top* (London: Paperbooks Ltd).

Courtenay-Smith, Natasha (2016), *The Million Dollar Blog* (London: Piatkus).

Covey, S. R. (2005), *The 7 Habits of Highly Effective People* (New York: Simon & Schuster).

Cuddy, Amy (2016), *Presence* (London: Orion).

Culpin, Vicki (2008), 'From Goldfish to Elephant – Make Your MARC in Business', *360 The Ashridge Journal* (Spring): 1–5.

Culpin, Vicki and Whelan, Angela (2009), 'The Wake-up Call for Sleepy Managers', *360 The Ashridge Journal* (Spring 2009): 1–4.

Defoe, Daniel (1726), *The Complete English Tradesman* (London).

Douglas, Kate (2016), 'Intelligent without Design', *New Scientist Magazine*, Issue 3066. Available online: https://www.newscientist.com/article/mg22930660-100-evolution-learn-natural-selection/ (accessed 30 June 2016).

Duhigg, Charles (2012), *The Power of Habit* (London: Heinemann).

Dunlop, Jocelyn O. (1912), *English Apprenticeship & Child Labour* (New York: Macmillan).

Emmons, Robert A. (2008), *Thanks!* (Boston, MA: Houghton Mifflin).

Fey, Tina (2012), *Bossypants* (London: Sphere).

Fletcher, P. C., Happé, F., Frith, U., Bakera, S. C., Dolana, R. J., Frackowiaka, R. S. J. and Frith, C. D. (1995), 'Other Minds in the Brain: A Functional Imaging Study of "Theory of Mind" in Story Comprehension', *Cognition* 57 (2): 109–28.

Fox, Kate (2004), *Watching the English* (London, Hodder).

Frederiksen, L. W., Harr, E. and Montgomery, S. S. (2014), *The Visible Expert* (Reston, VA: Hinge Research Institute).

French, J. R. P. and Raven, B. (1959), 'The Bases of Social Power', in

Cartwright, D (ed.), *Studies in Social Power* (Ann Arbor, MI: University of Michigan Press).

Frost, Peter and Robinson, Sandra (1999), 'The Toxic Handler', *Harvard Business Review* (July–August): 97–106.

Gallup (2013), *State of the Global Workplace* (Washington, DC: Gallup).

Gambetta, D. and Hertog, S. (2007), 'Engineers of Jihad' Sociology Working Papers 2007-10, Department of Sociology, Oxford University. Available online: http://www.sociology.ox.ac.uk/materials/papers/2007-10.pdf (accessed 30 June 2016).

Gladwell, Malcolm (2008), *Outliers* (London: Little, Brown & Co.).

Goethe, J. W. von (1970 [1840]), *Theory of Colours* (Cambridge, MA: MIT Press).

Goldsmiths' Company (1561), *Court Minute Book* K(i), 161.

Goleman, D. (2000), 'Leadership That Gets Results', *Harvard Business Review* (March–April): 78–90.

Goleman, Daniel (1996), *Emotional Intelligence* (London: Bloomsbury).

Goleman, D., Boyatzis, R. and McKee, A. (2002), *The New Leaders* (London: Little, Brown & Co.).

Granholm, E., Asarnow, R. F., Sarkin, A. J. and Dykes, K. L. (1996), 'Pupillary Responses Index Cognitive Resource Limitations', *Psychophysiology* 33 (4): 457–61.

Grint, Keith (2005), *Leadership* (Basingstoke: Palgrave Macmillan).

Hamel, Gary (1996), 'Strategy as Revolution', *Harvard Business Review* (July–August): 69–82.

Heifetz, R., Grashow, A. and Linsky, M. (2009), *The Practice of Adaptive Leadership* (Boston, MA: Harvard Business Press).

Heron, John (1970), 'The Phenomenology of Social Encounter – the Gaze', *Philosophy & Phenomenological Research* XXXI:2: 243–64.

Heron, John (1990), *Helping the Client* (London: Sage).

Heron, John (1993), *The Facilitators' Handbook* (London: Kogan Page).

Hilbert, M. and López, P. (2011), 'The World's Technological Capacity to Store, Communicate, and Compute Information' *Science* 332 (6025) 60–5.

Huffington, Arianna (2016), *The Sleep Revolution* (London: W. H. Allen).

Itten, J. (1970), *The Elements of Colour* (New York: Van Nostrand Reinhold Company).

Jacobsen, Mary (1999), *Liberating Everyday Genius* (New York, Ballantine).

Jamieson, J., Mendes, W. B., Backstock, E. and Schmader, T. (2010), 'Turning the Knots in Your Stomach into Bows: Reappraising Arousal Improves Performance on the GRE', *Journal of Experimental Social Psychology* 46 (1): 208–12.

Jiwa, M., Millett, S., Meng, X. and Hewitt, V. M. (2012), 'Impact of the Presence of Medical Equipment in Images on Viewers' Perceptions of the Trustworthiness of an Individual On-Screen', *The Journal of Medical Internet Research* 14 (4). Available online: http://www.jmir.org/2012/4/e100 (accessed 30 June 2016).

Kassam, K. S., Koslov, K. and Mendes, W. B. (2009), 'Decisions Under Stress: Stress Profiles Influence Anchoring and Adjustment', *Psychological Science* 20 (11): 1394–99.

Kipling, Rudyard (1982), *Just So Stories* (London: Piccolo).

Kleiner, Art (2003), 'Are You In With the In Crowd?', *Harvard Business Review*, 81(7): 86–92.

Konnikova, Maria (2016), 'Resilience and How To Learn It', *New Yorker*, 11 February. Available online: http://www.newyorker.com/science/maria-konnikova/the-secret-formula-for-resilience (accessed 30 June 2016).

Lally, P., Jaarsveld, C. H. M. van, Potts, H. W. W. and Wardle, J. (2010), 'How Are Habits Formed: Modelling Habit Formation in the Real World', *European Journal of Social Psychology* 40 (6): 998–1009.

Lammers, J., Dubois, D., Rucker, D. D. and Galinsky, A. D. (2013), 'Power Gets The Job: Priming Power Improves Interview Outcomes', *Journal of Experimental Social Psychology* 49 (4): 776–9.

Lane, Joan (1996), *Apprenticeship in England, 1600–1914* (London: UCL Press).

Levitin, Daniel (2014), *The Organized Mind* (London: Penguin).

Liu, A., Tipton, R., Pan, W., Finley, J., Prudente, A., Karki, N., Losso J. and Greenway, F. (2014), 'Tart Cherry Juice Increases Sleep Time in Older Adults With Insomnia', *The FASEB Journal* 28 (1), Supplement 830.9. Available online: http://www.fasebj.org/content/28/1_Supplement/830.9 (accessed 30 June 2016).

Machiavelli, N. (1999), *The Prince* (trans. George Bull) (London: Penguin).

MacIntyre, Alasdair (2003), *After Virtue* (London: Duckworth).

Maister, D. H., Green, C. H. and Galford R. M. (2000), *The Trusted Advisor* (New York: Free Press).

McGurk, H. and MacDonald, J. (1976), 'Hearing Lips and Seeing Voices' *Nature* 264 (5588):, 746–8.

Minto, Barbara (1987), *The Pyramid Principle* (London: Pitman).

Moser-Wellman, Annette (2002), *Five Faces of Genius* (New York: Penguin).

Murphy, Nora A. (2007), 'Appearing Smart: The Impression Management of Intelligence, Person Perception Accuracy, and Behavior in Social Interaction', *Personality & Social Psychology Bulletin* 33 (3): 325–39.

Newport, Cal (2016), *Deep Work* (London: Piatkus).

Oatley, Keith (1999), 'Why Fiction May Be Twice as True as Fact: Fiction as Cognitive and Emotional Simulation' *Review of General Psychology* 3 (2): 101–17.

Ochsner, K. N. and Gross, J. J. (2005), 'The Cognitive Control of Emotion', *Trends in Cognitive Sciences* 9 (5): 242–9.

Phelps, E. A. (2006), 'Emotion and Cognition: Insights from the Study of the Human Amygdala', *Annual Review of Psychology* 57: 27–53.

Ramlakhan, Nerina (2010), *Tired But Wired* (London: Souvenir Press).

Rollins, H. E. (ed.) (1958), *The Letters of John Keats Volume 1* (Cambridge: Cambridge University Press).

Rose, Martin (2015), 'Immunising the Mind – How can education reform contribute to neutralising violent extremism?', British Council. Available online: https://www.britishcouncil.org/sites/default/files/immunising_the_mind_working_paper.pdf (accessed 30 June 2016).

Sandberg, Sheryl (2015), *Lean In* (London: W. H. Allen).

Savage, Sara and Boyd-MacMillan, Eolene (2011), *The Human Face of Church* (Norwich: Canterbury Press).

Sayers, Dorothy L. (2004), *Letters to a Diminished Church* (Nashville, TN: Thomas Nelson).

Sennett, Richard (2009), *The Craftsman* (London: Penguin Books).

Singer, Emily (2016), 'New Evidence for the Necessity of Loneliness', *Quanta Magazine*, 10 May. Available online: https://www.quantamagazine.org/20160510-loneliness-center-in-the-brain/ (accessed 30 June 2016).

Smith, Charles E. (1994), 'The Merlin Factor: Leadership and Strategic Intent', *Business Strategy Review* 5 (1): 67–83.

Solomon, Robert C. (2003), 'Victims of Circumstances? A Defense of Virtue Ethics in Business', *Business Ethics Quarterly* 13 (1): 43–62.

Stacey, R. D. (2002), *Strategic Management and Organisational Dynamics* (Harlow: Prentice Hall).

Strack, F., Martin, L. L. and Stepper, S. (1988), 'Inhibiting and Facilitating Conditions of the Human Smile: A Nonobtrusive Test of the Facial Feedback Hypothesis', *Journal of Personality and Social Psychology*, 54 (5): 768–77.

Thomas, K. W. and Kilmann, R. H. (1974), *Thomas-Kilmann Conflict Instrument* (Palo Alto, CA: CPP).

Valiant, Leslie (2013), *Probably Approximately Correct* (New York: Basic Books).

Veale, Elspeth M. (1966), *The English Fur Trade in the Later Middle Ages* (Oxford: Oxford University Press).

Watzlawick, P., Weakland J. and Fisch, R. (1974), *Change* (New York: W. W. Norton & Co.).

Webb, Caroline (2016), *How to Have a Good Day* (London: Macmillan).

Weil, Simone (1951), *Waiting on God* (London: Routledge & Kegan Paul).

Weil, Simone (1952), *Gravity and Grace* (London: Routledge & Kegan Paul).

White, T. H. (1996), *The Once and Future King* (London: HarperCollins).

Whitmore, John (1996), *Coaching For Performance* (London: Nicholas Brealey).

Wilson, J. L. (2001), *Adrenal Fatigue* (Petaluma, CA: Smart).

Wiseman, R. (2009), *59 Seconds* (London: Pan).

Woods, Stewart (2012), *Eurogames* (Jefferson, NC: McFarland & Co.).

Wright, Angela (1995), *The Beginner's Guide to Colour Psychology* (London: Kyle Cathie).

York, Carol Beach (1984), *Miss Know It All* (London: Magnet).

Websites (all accessed 30 June 2016)

Apple design: http://uk.businessinsider.com/best-examples-apple-design-details-2015-4

Battery that doesn't run out: http://inhabitat.com/gold-nanowires-helped-researchers-design-a-battery-that-basically-lasts-forever/

Commander who ran aground: http://www.telegraph.co.uk/news/uknews/1404113/Commander-who-ran-aground-revealed-to-be-ships-saviour.html

Department for Education on character: https://www.gov.uk/
government/news/character-education-apply-for-2015-grant-
funding

Learning from Formula 1: http://news.bbc.co.uk/1/hi/technology/
7934857.stm

Idea Stores: http://www.ideastore.co.uk/

Social Mobility Commission on brown shoes: https://www.gov.uk/
government/uploads/system/uploads/attachment_data/file/
549994/Socio-economic_diversity_in_life_sciences_and_
investment_banking.pdf

Sumptuary law: http://elizabethan.org/sumptuary/who-wears-what.
html

Acknowledgements

This book is a hymn to a decade spent at Ashridge with some extraordinary colleagues. I should like in particular to thank the Future Leaders family, who are legion. The original team: Phil Hodgson, Melissa Carr, Jon Teckman, Margaret de Lattre, Barbara Banda and Sonia Gavira. Ellen Whitby, Lorraine Ellis, Dee Cullender, Nicki Sharples, Lynn Fawcus-Robinson and the army of co-ordinators down the years who wrestled with the logistics and are wrestling still. Megan Reitz and Chris Nichols, who ran the programme together for so many years. Core faculty Ange Muir, Kate Charlton, James Morrison, Vicki Culpin, Lynn Lilley, Ronnie Burke and the stalwarts who ran so many of the simulations with me. Our excellent supporting cast: Toby Roe, Mark Pegg, Paul Davies, Brian Worsfold, Andy Plumbly, Sian Rogers, Ange Jowett, the film crews and media, the librarians and everyone we roped in at the last minute each time to help. Sarah Cartwright, Nick Deal and the team at React who faithfully supported us throughout. Peter Blacker and Umbanda for the wholly necessary drumming after every one. Eddie Blass for her help writing up the original research, Ellen Pruyne for kicking off the Harvard research, and Professor Patricia Riddell from Reading for partnering with us on the neurobiology research. Lee Waller for managing the research programme, and John Neal for handling the heart monitoring. All our research guinea pigs for being so game, and George Horn for validating the templating effect. And, chiefly our clients, for taking the risk and letting us run the simulation for them. Particularly, in the early days, FCO, IDeA, Tesco and many others since then.

In writing the book, I have had lots of help with sources. Lt Col. Mervyn Bassett, the Beadle at the Skinners' Company; Eleni Bide at the Goldsmiths Library and Helen Dobson at Goldsmiths Centre; Patricia Riddell and Lee Waller on the neurobiology; and it was the lovely Monica Price, Head of Earth Collections, Oxford University Museum of Natural History who identified my font. Imogen Russon and Mark Taylor helped sharpen my thinking, and Ann O'Brien and Toby Roe gave me invaluable advice. Ronnie Burke, Sarah Cartwright, Natasha Courtenay-Smith, Vicki Culpin and Paul Davies helped me with exercises. Phil Hodgson, Paul Davies, Jonnie Noakes, Mark Pegg, Alice Poole, Jon Coldridge and Nathan Percival read my drafts and improved them. And Old Gordonstonian Andrew Packard told me about *amae*. Thanks to you all.

Leadersmithing as an idea emerged as part of my attempt to earth our research findings, so I am particularly grateful to Fiona Cameron at the Clore Leadership Programme for allowing me the space to develop some of the practicalities in this approach, and to the Clore Short Course alumni who have helped my thinking on it with their whole-hearted involvement and searching questions.

For this book, I have had kind permission to use materials from Daniel Goleman, Lauren Bacon, Sir John Whitmore and Gallup 12. I owe a deep debt of gratitude to all my Ashridge colleagues and clients for what I have learned, both with them and from them, over the years. Your name should probably be here, too – it is, in my heart.

Eve Poole

Index